QUICK CRAFTS

FOR PARENTS
WHO THINK THEY
HATE CRAFT

EMMA SCOTT-CHILD

"Practising an art, no matter how well or badly, is a way to make your soul grow, for heaven's sake. Sing in the shower. Dance to the radio. Tell stories. Write a poem to a friend, even a lousy poem. Do it as well as you possibly can. You will get an enormous reward. You will have created something."

KURT VONNEGUT,
A MAN WITHOUT A COUNTRY

CONTENTS

PLAY WITH IT

WEAR IT

SPRUCE IT UP

USEFUL THINGS

Craft has got a bad rep. It's for people who knit their own knickers and eat glitter for breakfast.

I believe that everyone can glean some joy from craft. Even if it's crooked, even if it falls apart tomorrow. It's the act of creating something that is good for the soul.

Creativity is all around us. When you cook dinner, when you put on an outfit, whenever you make decisions, it's there.

I have hosted craft workshops for years and have found that there are two types of people: those who identify themselves as 'crafty', and those who think they are rubbish at anything creative, but they still get stuck in to entertain their kids.

What I have found is that the people who believe they are less creative get the most enjoyment out of creating something – but they are less likely to start a project because they feel daunted.

I hope that this book gives you a new perspective on creativity and craft. Make it wonky and make it out of things that might usually be thrown away. It doesn't have to be Pinterest-worthy. Make it just for the sake of making.

If we keep it simple and remove the idea of perfection, it feels more achievable.

The key things that stop people from getting creative are time and mess. So in writing this book I made a few rules for myself:
+ No messy painting
+ No sewing
+ No special equipment
+ And most of all NO GLITTER!

These projects are quick, but they are also jumping-off points for adventures that last a little longer.

You might not have the time to spend all afternoon crafting, but you might have ten minutes to make some paper monsters that are the start of a monster adventure which lasts the rest of the day. Once you've made a project together, you can set the kids off on a journey playing with it, wearing it, or hanging it up for everyone to see.

Let's get started

WHY ARE WE DOING CRAFT?

All the projects in this book are designed to get our brains thinking creatively. Making, decorating and playing help us to notice aspects of design in the world around us: how objects work, the harmony of combining certain colours, how shapes can become faces and how to communicate visually. Craft can teach us how to approach the world in a problem-solving way.

I'd like this book to be a bit like a recipe book. You could try one of these projects in the same way that you might flick through a baking book and make a cake on a rainy afternoon. And just as you may have all the ingredients for a cake already there in your kitchen, you probably already have most of the things you'll need for a craft project at home.

The main thing is that it's something to do together with your child. Younger ones might only contribute with a bit of sticking, but the end result will be the same — that 'look what we made!' moment at the end.

HOW LONG WILL IT TAKE?

The projects will take different amounts of time depending on the age and number of kids that you're working with. I have included little clocks next to the project titles so you can see that some are quite quick, while others — towards the back of each chapter — are longer, rainy afternoon projects.

WHO DOES WHAT?

The age range for these projects is roughly four to eleven years old, but even children too small to do any of the projects will benefit from watching someone do them and can help with sticking and stamping.

I have included sections in the instructions that are marked as *GROWN-UP JOBS*. These are things that might need extra care, like using a craft knife or superglue.

Older kids (8+) might help a younger child or get on with the projects on their own. Be sure to tell them why the grown-up jobs are important, so they know to ask an adult to do these parts, or to supervise.

Although most of the photos show my hands doing the projects, most steps can be completed by the kids themselves. You know your child's abilities best, so encourage them to do the steps that you think they can manage. They might surprise you with their skills, given the opportunity.

Remember, nothing needs to be perfect; having a go and making something wonky is a great achievement in itself.

You don't need to be a craft nerd to have all the crafty bits. Most of the materials in this book might already be in your home.

As a designer, I often take a sideways glance at objects and think about how they could be used in different ways. The best things to use for craft are already lying around the house waiting to be reborn. The cupboard under the sink is full of goodies and so is the recycling bin.

The next few pages are a guide to all the bits you'll need for the projects. You'll find most of the items already around your house. But everything in here can be bought from the supermarket, the newsagent or the pound shop.

KITCHEN

Plastic bottles

Fork

Chopsticks

Toothpicks

Foil

Skewers

Popsicle sticks

Tea towel

Dried pasta

Paper cups

Paper plates

Sponges

Wooden pegs

Rubber gloves

HARDWARE

Gaffer tape

Masking tape

Craft knife

Superglue

STATIONERY

Scissors   Stapler

Glue stick   Felt-tip pens

Chalk pen   Drawing pins

Markers   Elastic bands

Pencils   Sticky tape

Ruler   Sticky dots

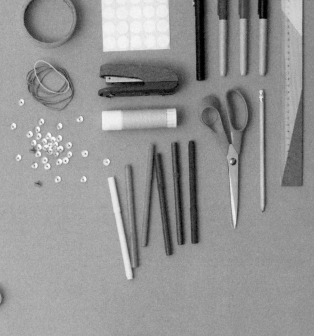

BATHROOM

Loo rolls

Tissue box

Cotton balls

Dental floss

Nail scissors

Nail polish

GARDEN

Flowerpot

Plants

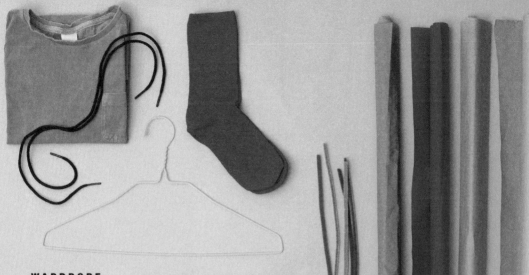

WARDROBE

T-shirts

Shoelaces

Socks

Coathangers

CRAFTY BITS

Polystyrene balls	Washi tape
Pipe cleaners	Wool
Tissue paper	PVA glue
Brown paper	White paint
String	Felt

CHAPTER 1

PLAY WITH IT

Projects to spark
creative play

PAPER MONSTERS

If you've ever made a mistake and scrunched up a ball
of paper, you've accidentally made a great starting point
for a funny little monster.

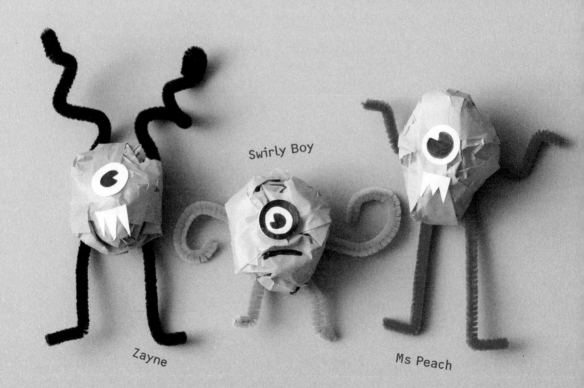

Swirly Boy

Zayne

Ms Peach

These guys are a great way to spark creative play and to look at how simple changes in shapes and colours can form characters.

Once you have your monster gang, you can give them names, think about what their specialist monster skills might be, and if you're feeling really fancy you could make them a hotel in a shoebox.

Petey
Blink-Blink

Mr Scufflesnatch

Sonya Sassbum

YOU WILL NEED

Paper – tissue, newspaper, wrapping paper, foil, etc.

Pipe cleaners for legs and arms

Tape – coloured washi tape looks great, or masking tape or Sellotape will work too

Sticky dots for eyes, or you could cut out circles of paper and glue them on

Felt-tip pen

Scissors

INSTRUCTIONS

1. Scrunch your paper into a ball. I used tissue paper for this one.

2. Wrap some tape around the ball of paper so it doesn't unravel.

3. Bend some pipe cleaners for arms and legs. Then trim them with scissors if you need to.

4. Tape the pipe cleaners onto the back of the monster.

5. Draw some eyes on the sticky dots, or cut out some circles of paper for eyes. Remember, some monsters only have one eye, others have loads!

6. Cut out any other features like fangs, eyebrows, or maybe a moustache.

7. Stick them on your monster to make its face.

8. Now you can give your monster a name and think of all its scary skills. Make lots of monsters in different shapes and sizes!

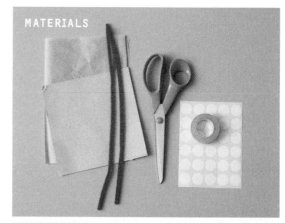

MATERIALS

1.

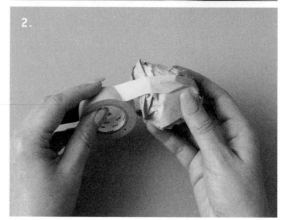

2.

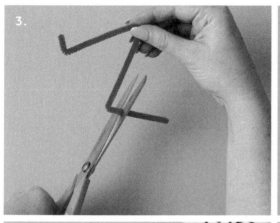

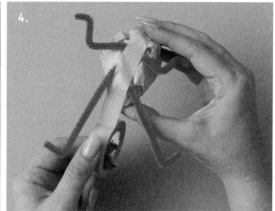

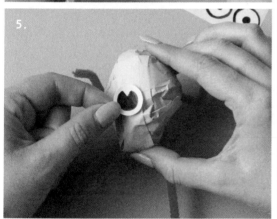

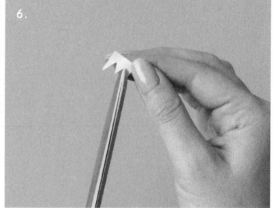

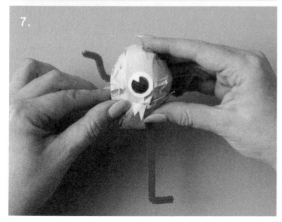

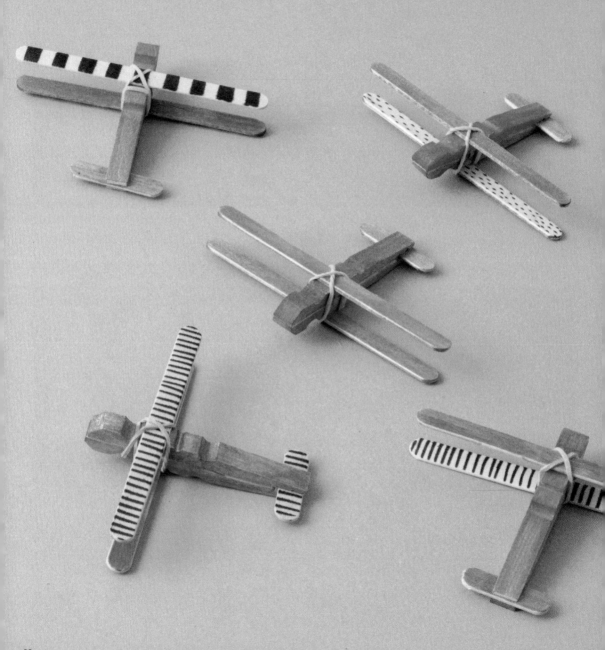

POPSICLE PLANES

These little planes are made just from wooden pegs, popsicle sticks and
an elastic band. If that isn't the perfect excuse to eat some ice lollies,
I don't know what is!

YOU WILL NEED

3 x popsicle sticks

1 x wooden peg

1 x elastic band

Felt-tip pens

Scissors

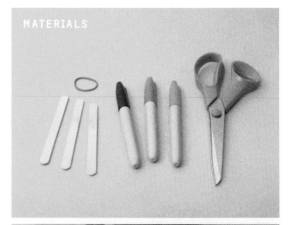

INSTRUCTIONS

1. Pull apart the wooden peg, then colour the pieces with the felt-tip pens.

2. Put the peg pieces together back-to-back, with the straight edges touching to form the body of the plane.

3. Place a popsicle stick on top of the plane's body and wrap the elastic band around the stick and the body, twisting the band so you end up with an 'X' crossing over the top.

4. Flip the plane over and place the other popsicle stick in place. Wrap the elastic band around it – once again crossing it over so you end up with an 'X'. If your elastic band is long, you may need to wrap it around a few more times to make it nice and tight.

5. Snap a small piece off the last popsicle stick; this will be the tail.

6. *GROWN-UP JOB* Trim the tail piece with scissors to make the end smooth and round like the other end – I use the back of the scissor blades for this.

7. Add the tail by wedging it in at the end. You could glue it in place with some PVA glue if you want it to be super secure.

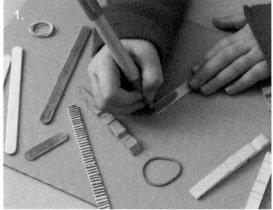

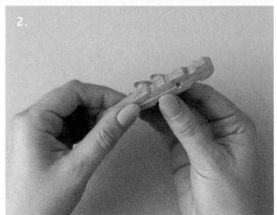

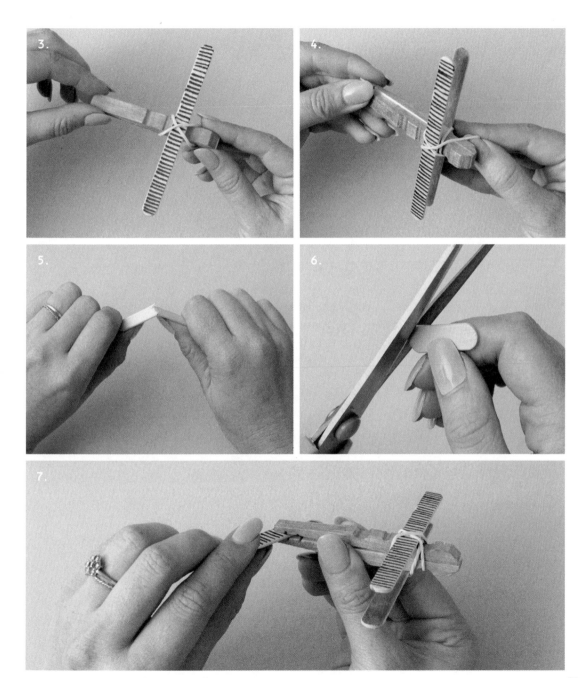

TEDDY FOR BLAST OFF

If your teddy is hoping to be an astronaut, he's going to need a space helmet*. This one is made out of a tissue box and it only takes about five minutes to make.

*May not be suitable for actual, real outer space.

YOU WILL NEED

A tissue box – or a small box that fits your teddy's head

Foil

Pipe cleaner

Scissors

A teddy – or doll, or rabbit, or monkey, or whomever would like to go to space

INSTRUCTIONS

1. Take the tissues out of the box. The hole that they come out of will be where teddy looks out of the helmet.

2. *GROWN-UP JOB* Cut another hole in the side of the box, next to the panel with the original hole, to put teddy's head through.

3. Place the box in the middle of a large piece of foil. Gather the foil and pull it up the side of the box and fold it around the rim of the window.

4. Press it down around the rim of the window to make it neat.

5. Curl the pipe cleaner around your finger, leaving one end straight.

6. *GROWN-UP JOB* Carefully make a hole in the top of the helmet with scissors.

7. Push the pipe cleaner through, bend, and tape it inside of the box.

8. Break the foil on the bottom, where the head hole is. Bend the foil around the opening, so it stays put. Now put it on your teddy's head!

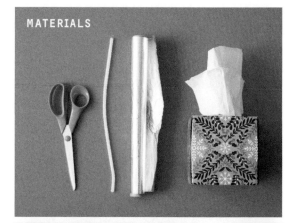

MATERIALS

1.

2.

PAPER PIRATE SWORDS

Arrr! Brace for swashbuckling
with these super-quick paper
pirate swords.

YOU WILL NEED

Tape

Scissors

Brown paper or newspaper

Cardboard — A recycled cardboard box is ideal

Something circular to trace around, like a saucer

INSTRUCTIONS

1. Roll up the paper, starting at one corner, rolling towards the opposite diagonal corner. It looks good if one end rolls down to a point. Tape the end so it doesn't unravel.

2. Flatten the wider (non-pointy) end up to about one third of the way up the full length.

3. Bend the flat part over to form a handle and tape the end to the main sword.

4. Trace around the saucer to make a circle on the cardboard. Cut it out.

5. *GROWN-UP JOB* Cut a small hole in the centre of the circle. Start with a small hole then slide it on to the sword. If you need to make the hole bigger, you can do it bit-by-bit until it is the right size to fit snugly on the sword at the base of the handle. It's tempting to go straight for the right-sized small hole, but it always needs to be smaller than you think. Now you're ready to be a pirate!

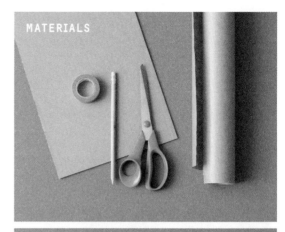

MATERIALS

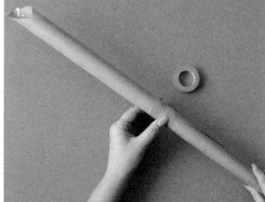

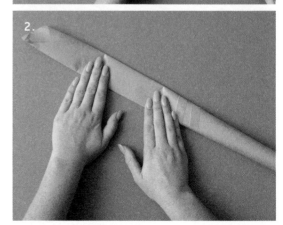

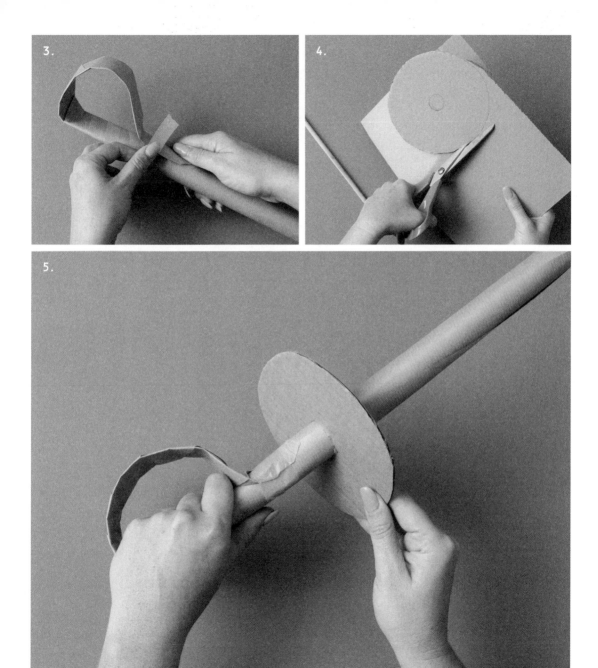

CAPTAIN HOOK'S HOOK ⏰

You can't have a pirate without a hook. This one only needs foil and a paper cup.

YOU WILL NEED

Foil

Paper cup

Scissors

INSTRUCTIONS

1. ***GROWN-UP JOB*** Pierce the bottom of the paper cup using scissors, to make a small hole in the centre.

2. Cut a square of foil. Place the cup in the centre of the square.

3. Fold the foil inside the cup until the whole cup is covered in foil.

4. Cut a new square of foil and shape it into a stick, a bit longer than a pencil.

5. Bend the foil stick into a hook shape, leaving a long, straight part at one end.

6. Poke the straight end of the hook through the foil on the bottom of the cup and through the hole.

7. Hold onto the straight end of the hook inside the cup and it's time for swashbuckling!

MATERIALS

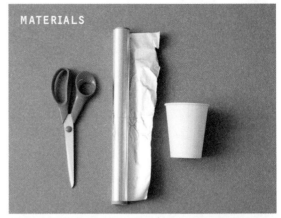

1.

2.

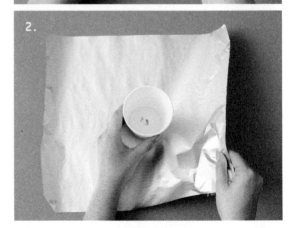

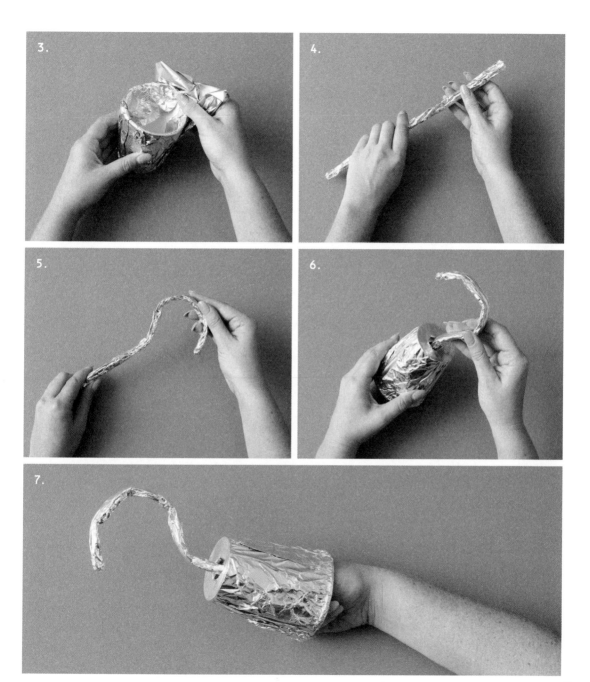

Fang

Polly

Trudie

Steve

Papa Jerry

PAPER PUPPETS ⏰⏰

These folded paper puppets take on all sorts of different characters depending on how you design their features.

Use them with the puppet theatre on page 42.

YOU WILL NEED

1 x sheet of A4/A3 paper

Glue stick

Felt-tip pens

INSTRUCTIONS

The basic structure of this is the same as the classic fortune-teller origami.

1. Make a square by folding a diagonal corner as shown. This will give you a guide of where to cut the paper to make a square.

2. Fold the square along both diagonals.

3. Open up the paper, then fold each corner into the middle, using the fold lines as a guide.

4. Turn it over and do the same again.

5. You should now have all corners folded into the middle.

6. Fold it in half.

7. Place your fingers inside and push it into a 3D-shape that splits into four parts.

8. Open it up again and add some glue to the triangle areas that are marked on the photo. These sections will stay together to make the shape of a face with a mouth.

9. Decorate the face with pens or paper features; you can add eyes, lips, fangs and eyelashes to make a funny character!

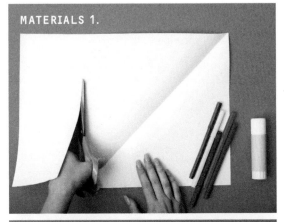

MATERIALS 1.

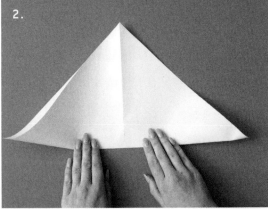

2.

3.

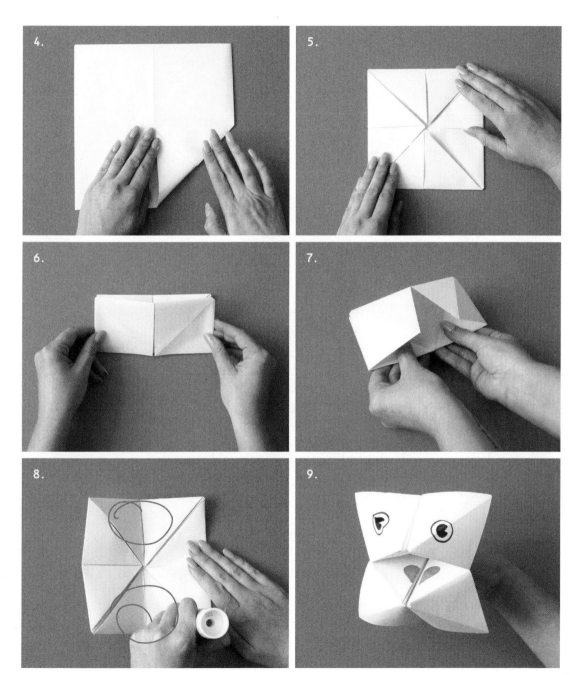

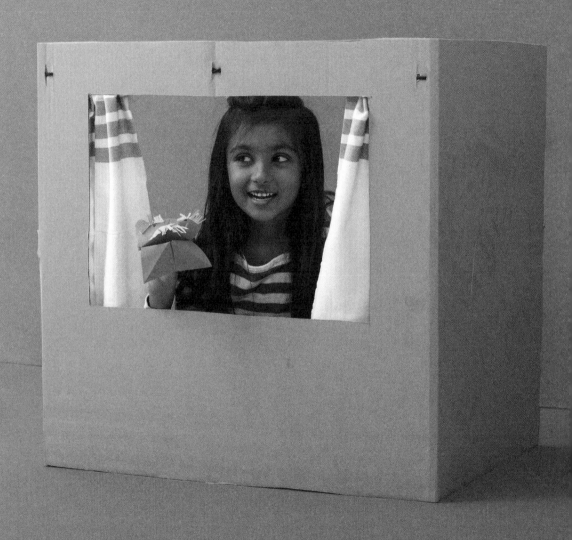

PUPPET THEATRE ⏰⏰

This puppet theatre is made from a cardboard box. It has curtains, but doesn't require any sewing; you can use tea towels, shoelaces and a stapler to create some curtains. And you can have the tea towels back afterwards when you're done with puppeteering.

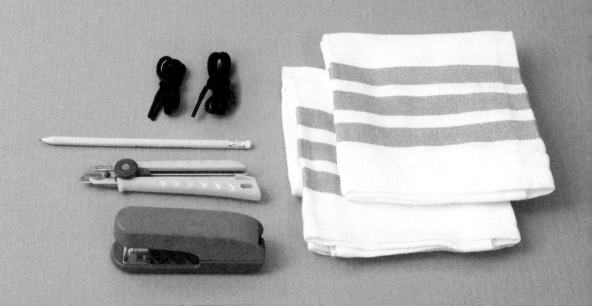

1 x large cardboard box

2 x shoelaces, or thick string

2 x tea towels

Craft knife

Stapler

Pencil

INSTRUCTIONS

1. Cut the box until you have three sides left with the widest in the centre.

2. Draw a large rectangle in the centre for the 'stage'.

3. ***GROWN-UP JOB*** Cut out the stage using the craft knife.

4. To make the curtains, lay the first tea towel out and lay a shoelace along the short edge about 3cm from the edge. Fold the edge of the tea towel over the shoelace like a hem, then staple the hem closed. Make sure that you don't accidentally staple the shoelace!

5. Scrunch up the curtain by pulling the shoelace carefully. Repeat with the second tea towel.

6. Make two small slits on either side of the stage window.

7. And make two more slits in the centre above the window.

8. Thread the shoelaces through the slits to hang the curtains.

9. Tie a bow in the centre and knots at the ends to hold them in place. The curtains simply move along the tea towels to open and close.

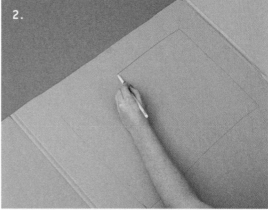

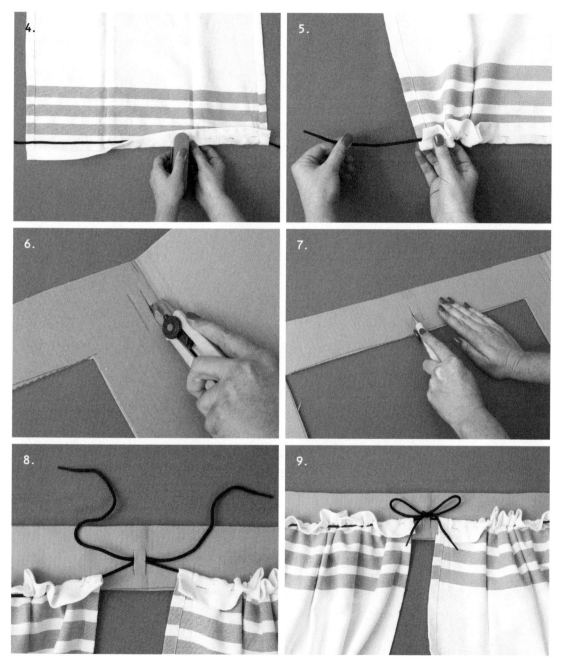

SQUIRTY BOTTLE WHALE

This little whale is great for bath times.
He's easy to make and you can make him squirt
through his blowhole.

YOU WILL NEED

1 x plastic juice bottle – a squarish smoothie bottle is ideal because it is slightly whale-shaped

Scissors

A permanent marker

Black gaffer tape

Food colouring (optional)

INSTRUCTIONS

1. Take off the lid, then wrap gaffer tape around the edge.

2. Squeeze the tape together to form a flat part to attach the tail to.

3. Stick a strip of tape (about 20cm long) centred along one side of the flat panel.

4. Stick another piece of tape to the other side to match.

5. Trim the corners to form a curved tail, then trim the end of the tail into a curvy 'V' shape, similar to a moustache.

6. *GROWN-UP JOB!!* Pierce a small hole in the bottle one third of the way up from the bottom.

7. Draw a face on the whale, a long line for his mouth and two dots for the eyes.

8. Fill the whale with water and add a little food colouring if you have any. Cover the hole with your finger while you fill it! Then give him a squeeze!

MATERIALS

1.

2.

SUPERHERO TEDDY

If your teddy is off on a crime-fighting adventure, they're going to need a mask and a cape. All you need is a sock!

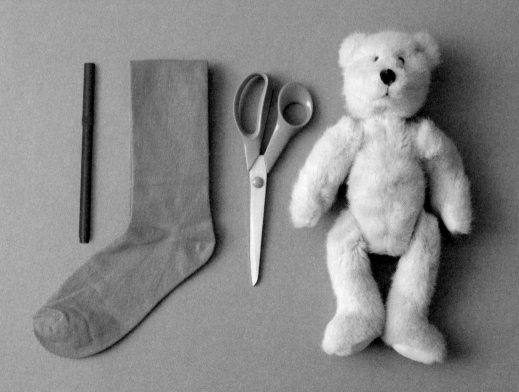

YOU WILL NEED

1 x small teddy – or rabbit, or doll,
or anything really!

1 x sock

Felt-tip pen or chalk to mark where to cut

Scissors

INSTRUCTIONS

1. Lay the sock flat and cut along the back
   of the ankle side until you get to the place
   pointed out on the photo. The toe of the
   sock will become the hood and the front
   of the cape.

2. Cut a triangle shape inwards, to half way
   across the sock as shown.

3. You will be left with two triangle pieces and
   the sock will form a cape and hood that can
   fit on the teddy's head.

4. Put the hood on the teddy's head.

5. Mark out where teddy's eyes are.

6. Mark out where teddy's ears are.

7. Take the hood off the teddy, then cut the
   marked places to form slits – don't cut a big
   hole at first, you can always make the holes
   larger if you need to.

8. Try the hood on the teddy and cut the eye
   holes some more if you need to. Now your
   teddy is off to fight for good/evil, depending
   on their preference!

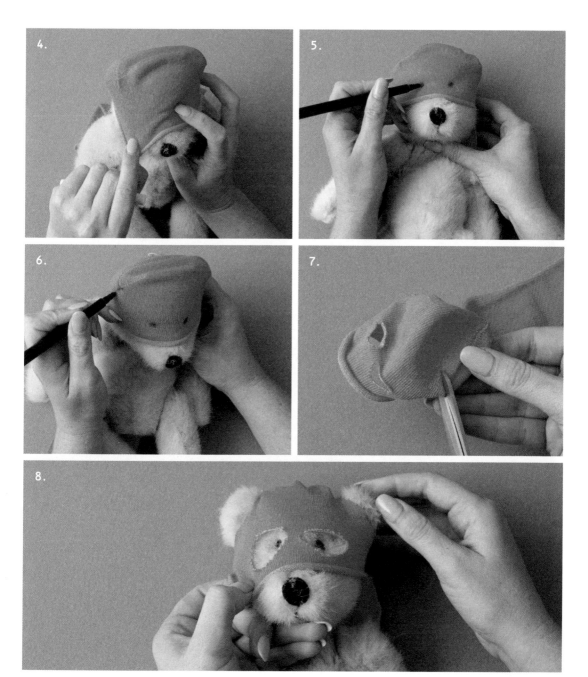

TOY
HAMMOCK

Toys need holidays too. This hammock for a toy uses a tea towel and doesn't involve sewing, so your dolly will be ready for a pina colada in no time.

This is a 'no sew' technique that's good for temporary crafts, which means you can unpick the staples and have your tea towel back after you've finished playing.

YOU WILL NEED

Tea towel

Two shoelaces – or thick string, wool or rope would also work

Stapler

INSTRUCTIONS

1. Take one of the shoelaces and tie a knot at one end.

2. Lay it out along one of the short edges of the tea towel, about 3cm from the edge of the fabric.

3. Fold the edge of the tea towel over to form a hem that encloses the shoelace.

4. Staple the hem together, making sure to avoid accidentally stapling the shoelace.

5. Gather the fabric together so it bunches up. Do the same at the other end of the tea towel.

Now you can tie the shoelaces between two chairs, and put a toy in the hammock for some serious relaxation time.

MATERIALS

1.

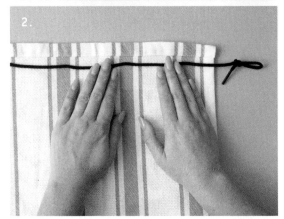

2.

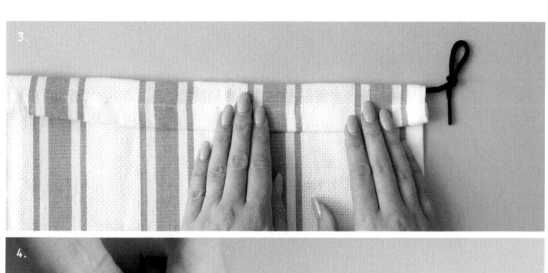

LOO ROLL
ROCKETS ⏰⏰

Get ready to blast off with these
loo roll rockets.

YOU WILL NEED

Loo roll inner tube

Bamboo skewer

Paper

Foil

Plastic bag or tissue paper

Masking tape

Scissors

Felt-tip pens

INSTRUCTIONS

1. Draw a circle on the paper by tracing around the roll of masking tape. Then cut the circle out.

2. Make one cut in the circle from the edge to the centre. Now overlap the edges to form it into a cone shape.

3. Cut a small piece of tape and secure the cone to the size you want it.

4. Cut some more pieces of tape and use them to attach the cone to the top of the loo roll to make your rocket shape.

5. Stuff the rocket full of scrunched-up foil. Poke the skewer into it through the cardboard.

6. Cut some zig-zag shapes out of a plastic bag or tissue paper. This will be the flames coming out of the rocket.

7. Scrunch the flames together at one end and use masking tape to stick them inside of the loo roll.

8. Draw on some windows, and any other decorations that you fancy.

MATERIALS

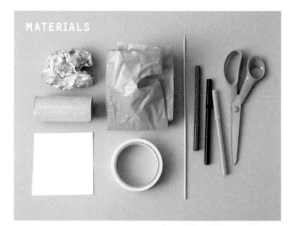

1.

2.

POMPOM MONSTERS

🕐

Each of these monsters is made from a whole ball of wool. You don't need
to wind the wool around a pompom template; you can just turn the whole
ball into a pompom without unravelling it!

YOU WILL NEED

1 x ball of wool (plus another colour, if you have one)

2 x cotton balls

Masking tape

Permanent marker

Scissors

INSTRUCTIONS

1. ***GROWN-UP JOB*** Tie a piece of wool or string very tightly around the middle of the ball of wool. Keep the ends very long because this is what you will hang your monster from. Make sure you use synthetic wool or string for this piece because the fibres are longer (natural wool won't be strong enough and may come apart)
   *This is a grown-up job just because it needs to be super tight.

2. Cut the loops of wool at one end of the ball so that they fray.

3. You don't need to be neat, just chop away at it until all the loops are cut.

4. Now do the same for the other end.

5. Now, when you hold it by the long piece of wool, you will have a big shaggy pompom.

6. Draw some circles on the masking tape for the eyes and cut them out.

7. Stick the eyes on to the two cotton balls.

8. Use a small piece of masking tape to stick the eye onto a couple of strands of wool.

9. Attach the other eye and now you have a shaggy monster!

GAFFER TAPE SUSHI

The laundry cupboard holds all the ingredients for this funny,
spongey sushi. Chop up bits of sponge, add some cotton wool and use
gaffer tape to roll it all together.

Experiment with different colours and textures to see what other
sorts of sushi you can make.

YOU WILL NEED

Gaffer tape

Cotton wool balls

Sponges of various colours

Paper plate – to make a prawn

Bubble wrap – to make salmon roe

Felt-tip pens

Scissors

INSTRUCTIONS

CLASSIC SUSHI ROLL

1. Start by unravelling a cotton ball into a long strip. Or if you're making a large piece of sushi, unravel a few. I have used three.

2. Cut two sponges into thin strips. Layer the sponge to look like different ingredients and roll it into a spiral.

3. Wrap the cotton wool around the edge of the sponge roll.

4. Wrap the whole roll in gaffer tape and cut the tape. This makes a roll as wide as the roll of gaffer tape, but you can make narrower rolls by using half the width of gaffer tape.

PRAWN NIGIRI

1. Cut out a prawn shape from the edge of the paper plate. The edge will bend up like a prawn tail. Colour it with a felt-tip pen.

2. Unravel a cotton wool ball into a long strip. Fold it into shape.

3. Cut a small, thin piece of gaffer tape.

4. Wrap the tape around the prawn and the cotton wool roll to make a nigiri!

2.

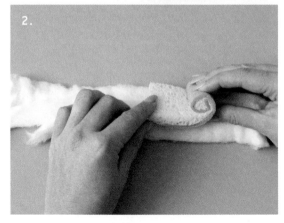

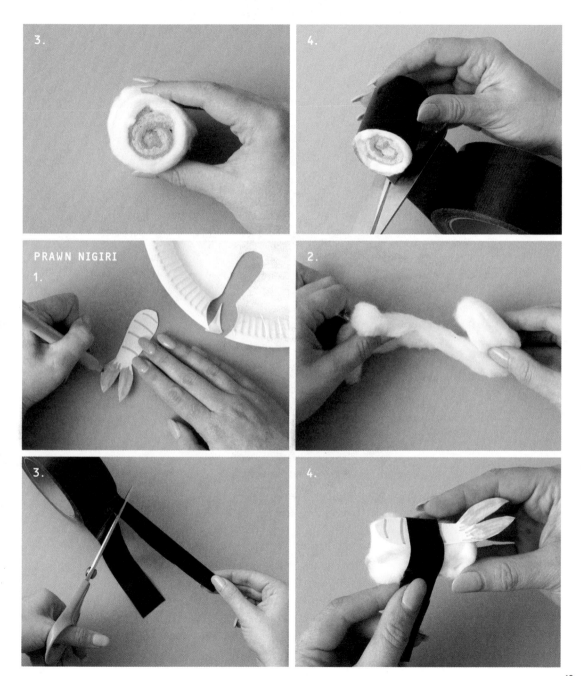

3.

4.

PRAWN NIGIRI
1.

2.

3.

4.

WOODLAND FRIENDS

It wouldn't be a kid's craft book without some loo roll animals, would it? Here is my take on a classic – some woodland friends: a badger, an owl and a fox.

By folding the top of the loo rolls down, we can create little ear shapes, and little strips of paper can create the distinctive markings for each of the animals.

YOU WILL NEED

Loo rolls

A4 sheet of white paper

Felt-tip pens – I used brown, grey and orange, but you could use any colours you like

Scissors

Glue stick

INSTRUCTIONS

1. Bend the top of a loo roll tube on one side.

2. Now do the same on the opposite side. This will make the little ear shapes.

BADGER

1. Cut three pieces of white paper out for the white markings as shown. Glue them on.

2. Draw on his eyes, an oval for his nose and add marks for his fur.

OWL

1. Cut two pieces of white paper out for the white markings: a heart for his face and a semi-circle for his tummy as shown. Glue them on.

2. Draw on his eyes, a small triangle for his beak and some feathers.

FOX

1. Cut four pieces of white paper out for his white markings and a tail as shown. Glue them on.

2. Draw on his eyes, a little heart for his nose, and some orange fur.

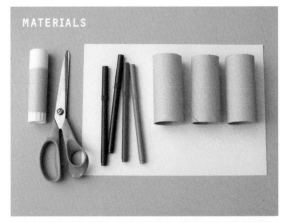

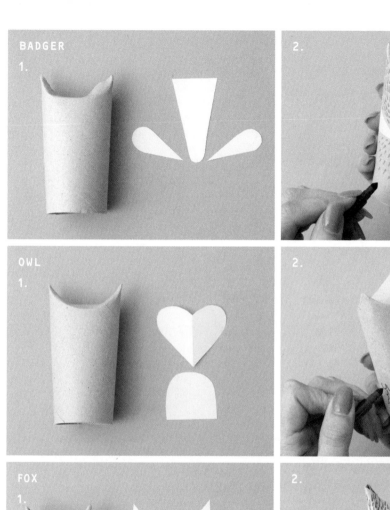

BADGER

1.

2.

OWL

1.

2.

FOX

1.

2.

A FRIENDLY PAPER
RATTLESNAKE

This friendly snake is made from sheets of paper turned into 3D shapes.
We filled the tail with rice so it rattles like a real rattlesnake.

YOU WILL NEED

A4 paper

Rice

Glue stick

Scissors

Felt-tip pens to draw the eyes

INSTRUCTIONS

1. To make the sections of the snake, you first need to make paper pockets, similar to paper bags. Glue along two edges of the paper — the long top edge and the short left-hand edge.

2. Fold into the centre on the left and right to form a paper pocket.

3. Add rice to the pocket; this will be your rattly tail end.

4. Glue along the inside edge of the pocket and join the sides together, so the creases touch.

5. This will form a 3D shape, a bit like a pyramid.

6. Make at least five pyramids, then glue them together, connecting them by the flat ends.

7. Cut a point at the front for the mouth.

8. Make a paper tongue by cutting out some paper into a tongue shape. Colour it red, or any colour you like. Then glue it inside the mouth.

9. Draw on two eyes with a pen. Your snake is ready to rattle!

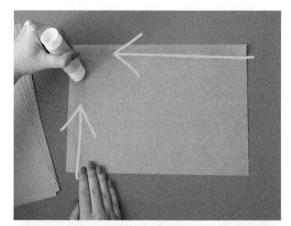

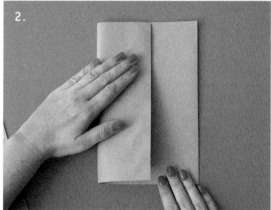

CLUCKING CHICKEN

This simple chicken makes a loud clucking noise which results in lots of giggles. It works because the cup acts like a speaker, amplifying the sound when you rub the sponge along the string.

Paper cup

Rubber glove – yellow works well

Sponge

String – cotton or plastic string will work

Tape – I used masking tape

Felt-tip pens

Scissors

INSTRUCTIONS

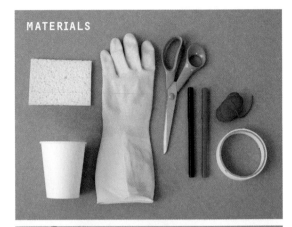

MATERIALS

1. ***GROWN-UP JOB*** Carefully pierce a hole in the bottom of the cup with scissors.

2. Feed about 40cm of string through the cup.

3. Tie a big knot in the string and tape it to the bottom of the cup so that when you pull it, it doesn't come through the hole.

4. Cut a small 3 x 5cm section off the sponge. Tie the piece of sponge to the other end of the string.

5. Chop the top half off the glove, so you have all the fingers (and not the thumb) in one piece.

6. Wrap the glove around the bottom of the cup to form the chicken's comb. Tape it onto the cup.

7. Draw on two eyes and a little triangle for the beak.

8. Now you can make it cluck! Make the sponge slightly moist, then fold it around the string. Pull along the string, gripping tightly. As it slides, it will make a loud clucking sound!

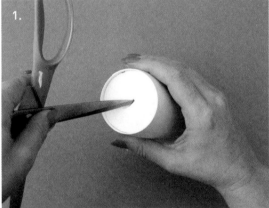

1.

2.

WOVEN PAPER CHESSBOARD

Make your own chess set by weaving pieces of black and white card to make the board. You could also use this board to play draughts if chess is too tricky.

We made our own chess pieces out of Lego™; it took a while to figure out the different values of the pieces but it is an interesting way to look at how shapes and characters can take on different meanings and values.

White card and black card, or if you'd prefer, you could use different colours — how about a pink and green chessboard?

Ruler

Scissors

Pencil

Tape

INSTRUCTIONS

1. Draw a square on the card that is the length and width of the length of your ruler. Cut the square out, but *IMPORTANT* leave some extra card along one edge.

2. Draw lines along the square to form eight equal strips. My ruler was the right width to just use the width of the ruler for the strips — lots of rulers are.

3. Do the same with the black card, but cut them all off so you have separate strips.

4. One by one, weave the black card in and out of the white card.

5. Push each strip to the top once you have woven it across.

6. Soon you will have a whole chessboard, which is 8 x 8 squares.

7. Trim off the excess ends.

8. Stick tape along each side of the board to hold the strips down. Fold the tape over so it covers the edge, then trim the excess tape off the corners.

MATERIALS

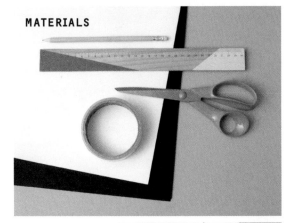

1.

2.

WEAR IT

Projects you can wear

FLAPPY BAT WINGS

This flappy bat is a super simple way to make a spooky
costume. All you need is one sheet of cardboard,
some rope and tape, and you're ready to scare
the neighbourhood.

YOU WILL NEED

1 x sheet of black cardboard

Some thick wool, rope or ribbon

A dinner plate – to trace around

Some chalk or a lead pencil

Some tape – any tape will do

Scissors

INSTRUCTIONS

1. Cut the card into two equal triangles by folding it in half from diagonal corner to corner, then cut along the fold.

2. Take one of the triangle pieces. Use the edge of the plate to draw three curves along the long edge of the triangle, starting at the bottom corner. Leave the end straight.

3. Cut out these curves to form a bat wing.

4. Place the batwing-shaped triangle on top of the uncut triangle and trace the same curves onto it.

5. Now cut the second batwing shape, and you will have two matching wings.

6. Stick on two small squares of tape to reinforce the holes for the rope, one in the corner, the other about 12cm below it.

7. ***GROWN-UP JOB*** Cut some holes through the tape and cardboard.

8. Thread wool, rope or ribbon through the holes into a big loop for the arm straps. Try the wings on and tighten the wool to the correct length so that they stay on your little bat.

MATERIALS

1.

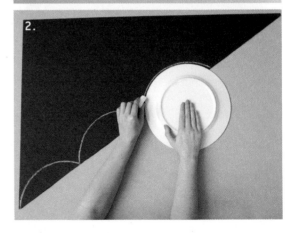

2.

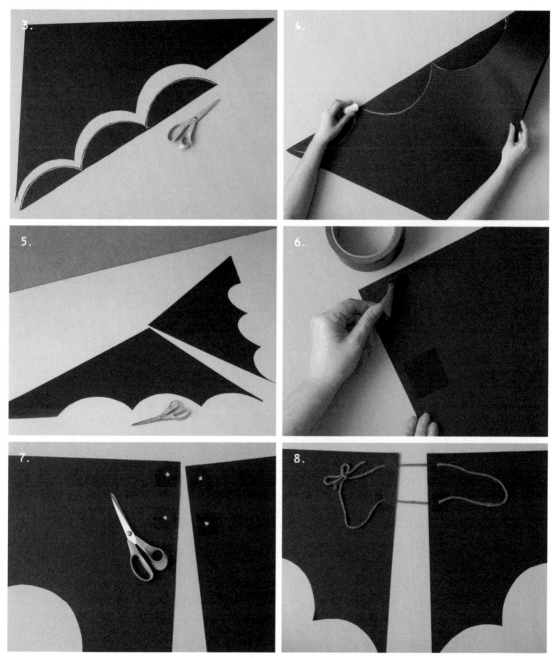

LEAF CROWNS

These leaf crowns are just made from real leaves. That's it! You don't need string, or scissors or anything else. Just leaves. So simple, you can make them while you're out and about in the park.

You can use autumn leaves, if it's that time of year, but you can also use green leaves. The main thing to look for when you're leaf hunting is that they are large enough, not too crispy to fold, and not too floppy to stand up straight.

YOU WILL NEED

Leaves. That's it!

INSTRUCTIONS

1. First take all the stalks off your leaves and set them aside. The stalks will hold the crown together.

2. Lay the first two leaves face down, overlapping. Fold the bottom of the leaves up to form the straight edge which will form the bottom edge of the crown.

3. Take one of your stalks and pierce it through both of the leaves where they overlap. Then take it back through the leaves through a second hole.

   The key to doing this is that the stalk goes through both leaves, both times that it pierces through. If your crown comes apart, it may not have pierced through both leaves.

4. Add the next leaf and attach it the same way. Continue doing this until you have a long chain of leaves to wrap around your head with a small overlap.

5. Once you have your whole crown, join it together with one final stalk.

6. If you're feeling fancy, make a centrepiece for the front. I used different coloured leaves, layered together.

7. Attach the centrepiece the same way using a stalk, piercing through all the layers of the crown on the front.

MATERIALS

1.

2.

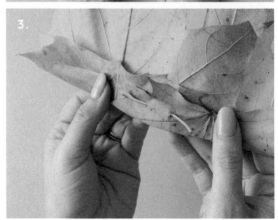

3.

ALIEN HEADBAND

⏰⏰

This is a fun way to upcycle a plain headband with a bit of an outer-space twist. You could wear it while your teddy goes to space with his helmet on page 26.

YOU WILL NEED

1 x plain headband

4 x polystyrene balls

4 x pipe cleaners

Tape – I used washi tape, but you could
also use masking tape or electrical tape

Scissors

PVA glue

Permanent marker pen

INSTRUCTIONS

1. Draw some black pupils on the polystyrene
   balls with the marker pen.

2. Put some PVA glue on the end of one
   pipe cleaner.

3. Carefully poke the gluey end of the pipe
   cleaner into the polystyrene ball.

4. Repeat with all the eyeballs and pipe
   cleaners. Trim the pipe cleaners with
   scissors; if they are quite long, they will
   be too floppy and won't stand upright.

5. Wrap the tape around the headband, starting
   at one end.

6. When you are about one third of the way
   around the headband, add one of the pipe
   cleaner eyeballs by placing it on the top
   of the headband and continue wrapping the
   tape around.

7. Continue along the headband, adding each
   pipe cleaner eyeball on as you go.

8. Bend the pipe cleaners so they stand upright.
   Now, take me to your leader!

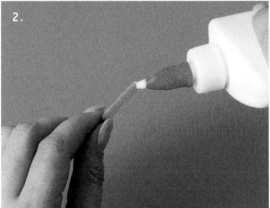

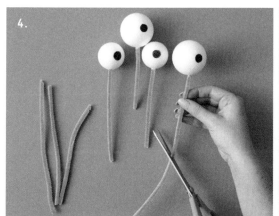

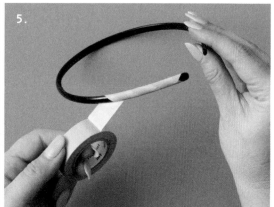

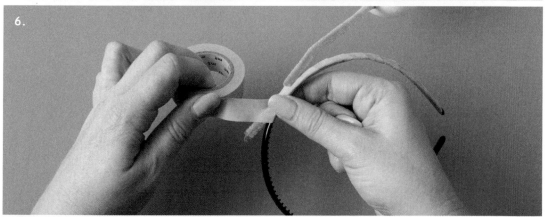

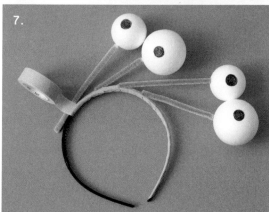

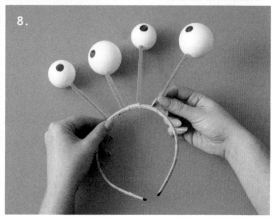

PLAYING CARD CROWNS

We always seem to lose cards from our packs of cards,
so I wanted to figure out something fun to do with the ones that are left.
These crowns are easy and fun to make and once you get started,
you can make endless designs with different combinations
of bends and joins.

How tall can you make your crown?
What would your king or queen name
be? See where your imagination
takes you.

Playing cards

Stapler

You could also use old business cards
if you have some that you don't need
any more

INSTRUCTIONS

1. Start by stapling about eight cards together
   to make a long strip.

2. Wrap it around your head to check the size.
   Staple the two ends of the strip together to
   form a loop.

3. Make another long strip and staple it from
   front to back, over the top of the crown.

4. To make a pointy top staple two cards back
   to back, then prise them apart and join the
   bottoms of the cards to the cross-band.

5. Fasten the strip over the crown, to form a
   cross across the crown with a pointy top.

6. To make a curvy king crown, bend two strips
   of cards into the centre and add some cards
   sticking up in the centre.

7. To make it stay put, bend a card at the bottom
   of the inward join.

8. Staple this card to the band that goes across
   the head.

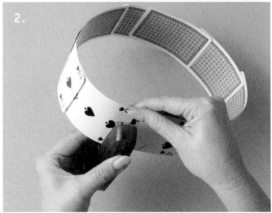

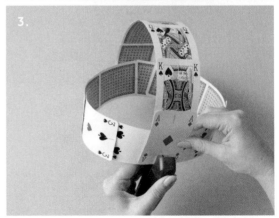

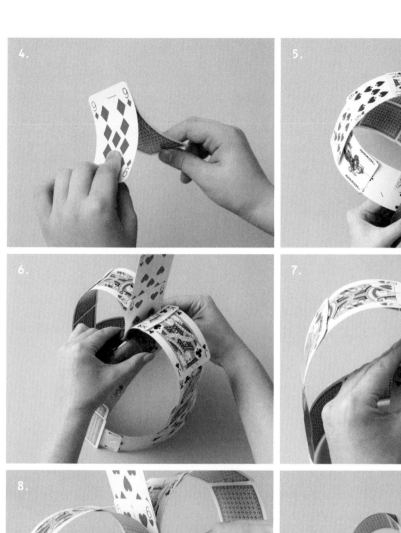

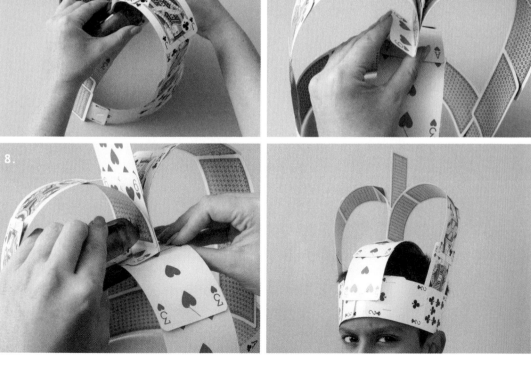

SKELETON MASK ♡ ♡

Boo! Get spooky with this
super-easy skeleton mask.
It's just made from a paper plate,
string and some masking tape.

YOU WILL NEED

1 x paper plate

Masking tape — to trace around and to use

A small circular object to trace around
— like a small roll of tape or a bottle top

String or wool

Scissors

Pen or pencil

INSTRUCTIONS

1. First imagine the plate is a clock and mark lines that are about 4cm long at 9, 11, 12, 1 and 3 o'clock.

2. Use the 9 and 3 o'clock markings as a guide and trace around the roll of masking tape to create two circles.

3. Trace around the bottle top to draw eyes.

4. Draw two straight lines from the masking tape circles, down to the curved ridge on the plate. These will form the sides of the mouth.

5. Cut the bottom section of the plate as shown, to make the face shape.

6. Cut a heart shape for the nose.

7. Add some small cuts for the teeth. Cut down the three lines on the top of the plate (at 11, 12 and 1 o'clock).

8. Overlap these sections to create a 3D forehead for the mask. Fasten them with pieces of masking tape.

9. Tape some wool or string to the sides so you can wear it as a mask.

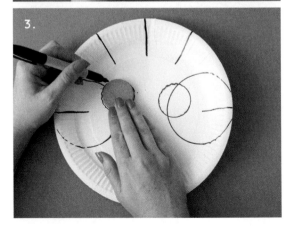

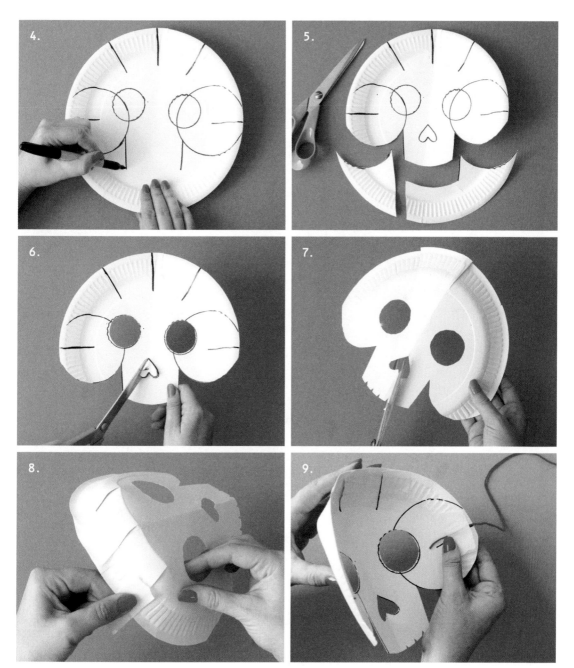

MACARONI NECKLACE

OK, so it's not technically macaroni, it's penne! When I think of macaroni necklaces, they are usually cute, but not very wearable. I wanted to see if I could make one I would actually wear.

I kept the design super simple and used nail polish to paint them and make them look lovely and shiny.

This project involves superglue and nail polish, so I wouldn't recommend it for anyone under five years old or you could end up in a sticky situation.

YOU WILL NEED

A chain or leather style necklace

2 x pieces of dry penne pasta

A straw — or some tightly rolled paper

Superglue

Nail polish

A glass

INSTRUCTIONS

1. Start by poking the straw through a piece of penne so that it stays on the end. This means you can paint it with nail polish without getting mucky fingers.

2. Paint one coat of nail polish on the first piece of pasta. Then leave it to dry by standing it in a glass. Once it has dried, do another coat. Do the same with the second piece of pasta.

3. *GROWN-UP JOB* Put some superglue around the end of one of the pieces of pasta.

4. Carefully stick the other piece of pasta on the end and hold the two pieces together for one minute (or until it feels like it has stuck).

5. Leave it to dry for about 10 minutes.

6. Thread the chain through your pasta pendant. Wiggle the pasta along to the centre of the chain. Now you can wear it!

   If you do end up permanently stuck to a piece of penne (!), the best way to come unstuck is to use nail polish remover which contains acetone, then wash your hands thoroughly with soapy water.

MATERIALS

1.

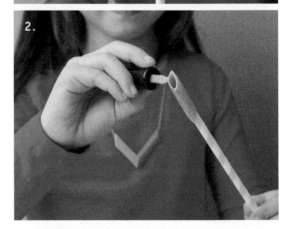

2.

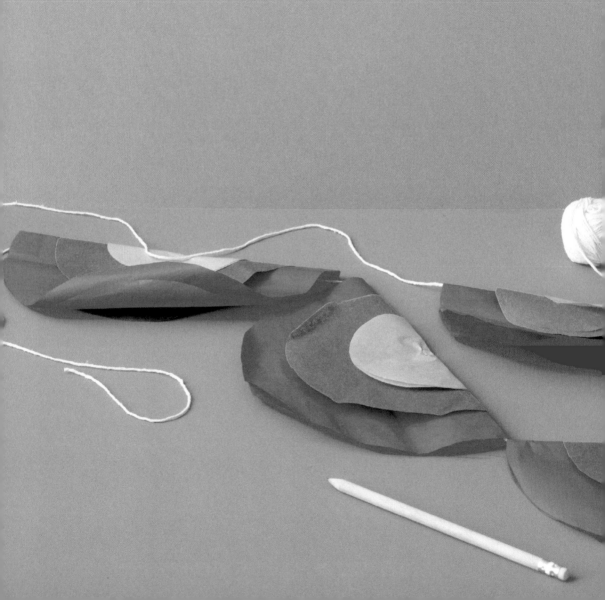

CHAPTER 3

SPRUCE IT UP

Projects to decorate your space

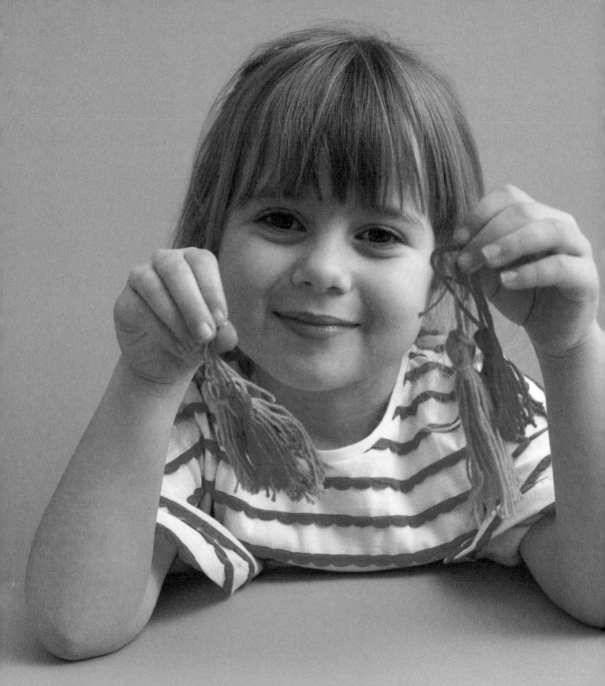

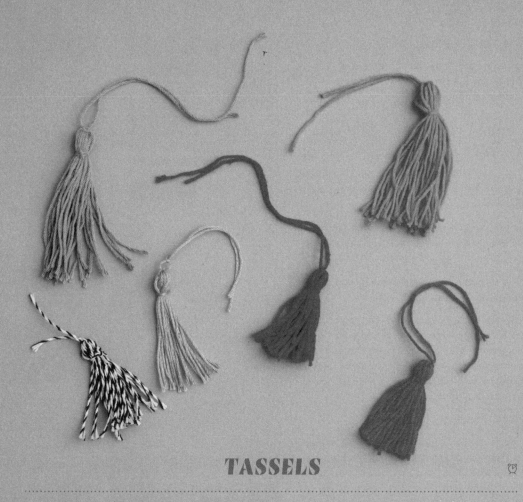

TASSELS

Tassels are a great way to make things feel fancy and a little bit festive, and they are really easy to make. You can use string, wool, embroidery thread, butcher's twine ... all sorts of threads. You can add them to lots of the projects in this book like the magic star and the moon wall hanging.

This version uses a card as a template, but you could make a really long tassel by using something larger like a take-away box lid.

YOU WILL NEED

String, wool or thread

A plastic card – like a credit card or library card. A cardboard card might not be rigid enough

Scissors

INSTRUCTIONS

1. Wind some string, wool or thread around the card. The more you wind it around, the more bushy the tassel will be.

2. Cut the yarn so that the beginning end and the final end finish on the same edge of the card. This will be the bottom of the tassel.

3. Slide a new piece of yarn between the wound thread and the card.

4. Pull this piece of yarn up to the top of the tassel (on the edge of the card), then tie it in a double knot so it holds all the wound yarn together. Keep this piece quite long – it will become the piece of yarn that the tassel hangs from.

5. Slide the whole thing off the card.

6. Take another piece of yarn and tie it around near the top of the tassel tightly with a double knot. Cut the dangling yarn off quite close to the knot.

7. Now cut the bottom loops of the tassel so that they form a nice, tassely fringe. Now you have a tassel!

8. If you want to make a longer tassel, use the longer length of the plastic card and follow the same instructions.

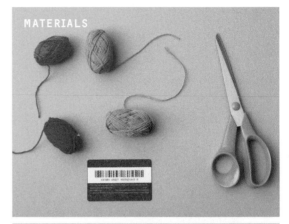

MATERIALS

1.

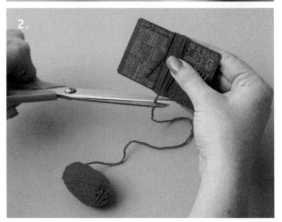

2.

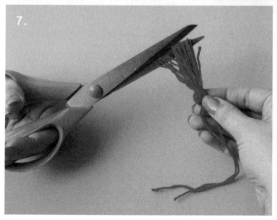

A FLOWERPOT FAMILY ⏰⏰

Make a family portrait from some flowerpots,
using plants for hair.

Think about the features of your family members' faces
and make a pot for each person. Drawing characters can
be daunting, but when we break it down into easy steps
we can create some fun faces and learn how different
shapes create different characters.

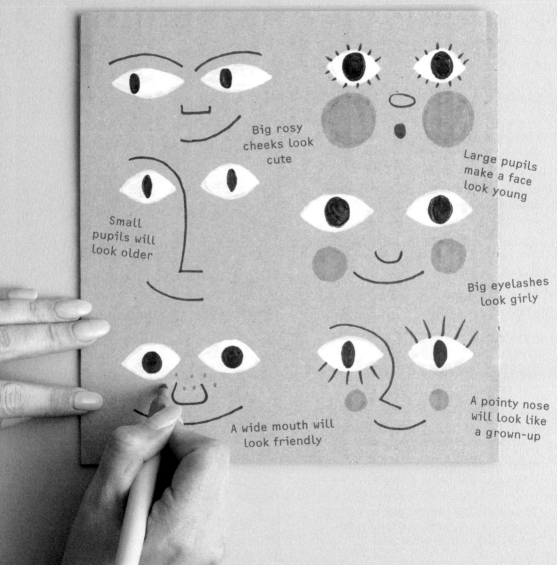

A slightly sideways smile looks like a smirk

A wide little oval for a nose will look like a kid

A tiny mouth looks like a baby

Big rosy cheeks look cute

Large pupils make a face look young

Small pupils will look older

Big eyelashes look girly

A wide mouth will look friendly

A pointy nose will look like a grown-up

YOU WILL NEED

Terracotta flowerpots

Plants and soil

White chalk marker, or Posca pen

Black permanent marker

A red or pink permanent marker

A pencil

INSTRUCTIONS

First practise drawing some faces on a piece of paper to get the right expression for each person. Have a look at the previous page for some tips on how to draw characters.

1. Once you know what you are going to draw, draw the outline of the eyes on a pot with a pencil.

2. Colour the eyes in with the white chalk marker or Posca pen. You might need to do another coat once it is dry.

3. Use the black permanent marker to draw on the nose and mouth.

4. Once the white eyes are dry, draw on the pupils, eyelashes and eyebrows in black.

5. Use the red or pink marker to draw on the rosy cheeks.

6. Add your plant! Depending on the type of plant you have, you may need to put some pebbles at the bottom of the pot for drainage.

7. Repeat with as many flowerpots as you like to make a living family protrait!

This project is probably best for indoor plants. The white chalk marker may not do very well outside in the rain.

MATERIALS

1.

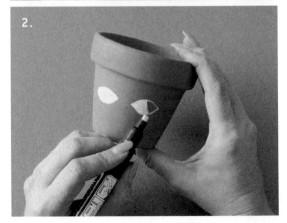
2.

PAPER FEATHERS ⏰⏰

These pretty feathers can be made using skewers, foil and plain white paper. You could also use coloured paper, but I like the white and silver because they look like feathers from angel wings ... or space seagulls perhaps!

They look really pretty hanging by a window where they will spin around in the breeze.

It takes lots of concentration to make all the small cuts, so this project is for people who are confident with scissors. It is also useful for practising focus and fine motor skills.

YOU WILL NEED

A4 white paper

Foil

Bamboo skewers or cocktail sticks

Glue stick

Scissors

String

INSTRUCTIONS

1. Take your piece of paper and completely cover it with glue.

2. Working fast, before the glue dries, place the skewer in the centre of the page, with the pointy end of it poking out of the bottom by about 4cm, like the quill of a feather. You could use a cocktail stick instead. Just stick it half on the page, half off, so it pokes out the bottom.

3. Cover the whole page in foil and press it down so it sticks all over the page. Cut the foil off the roll.

4. Fold the page in half, with the skewer in the centre of the fold.

5. Cut the folded paper into a feather shape, starting at the top.

6. Starting at the bottom end, cut thin fringing all the way up the length of the feather. The skewer will help to stop you cutting too far. If you have used a cocktail stick, be careful not to cut all the way to the end and accidentally chop it in half!

7. Once you have fringed the whole length, carefully open it up to make a feather.

8. If you want to hang it, tie some string onto the wooden quill with a double knot.

MATERIALS

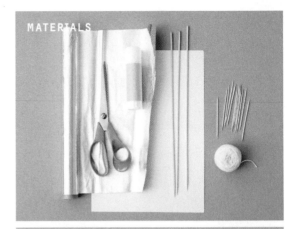

1.

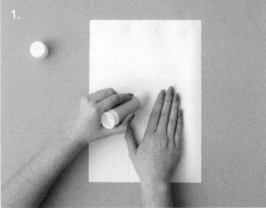

2.

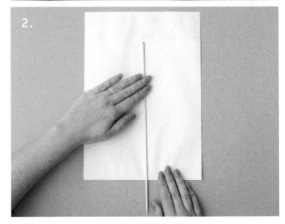

JUNGLE BUNTING

Welcome to the jungle ... inside
your house!

These leaves are simple to make using
green paper – or any colour really.
Just cut and fold them in a way
that makes them look like big
rainforest leaves.

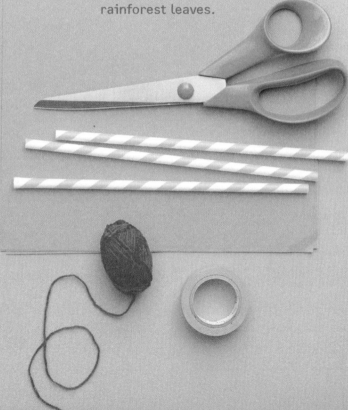

YOU WILL NEED

Coloured paper — one A4 sheet per leaf

Drinking straws

String or wool

Tape

Scissors

INSTRUCTIONS

1. Fold a sheet of paper in half lengthways. Cut it into a big leaf shape.

2. Here are some different shapes you could cut. I like to make them all a bit different.

3. This is what they look like once they are opened up.

4. Now fold the leaf on a diagonal and press down with your finger, only on the part of the fold leading from the central fold towards the outer edge of the leaf. Don't drag your finger all the way to the edge of the leaf.

5. Open the leaf, then repeat the same fold on the other side of the middle seam.

6. Keep doing this along the leaf so you have folds all the way along it.

7. Cut your straw into small sections.

8. Tape two sections to the back of each leaf, right at the top as shown.

9. Thread the string or wool through the straws. Make as many leaves as you like. Thread them together until you have a nice long chain of leaves.

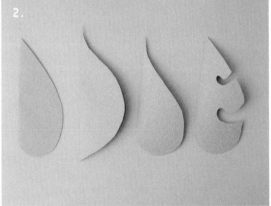

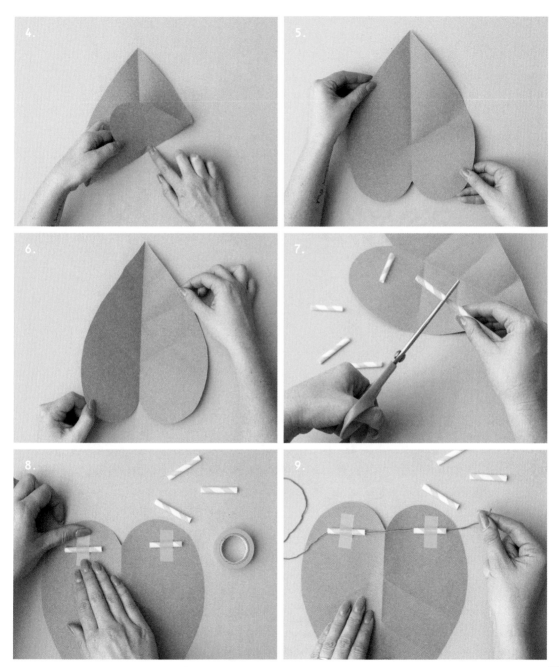

PAPER BAG STARS

These stars look tricky to make, but they are actually super easy. I have used them to decorate all sorts of events. They can be made with any type of paper bag — as long as it doesn't have a side wall built in. Any bag that is essentially made like a simple pocket is best.

I bought my bags from a newsagent; they were being sold as 'party bags'. You can also ask a sandwich or sweet shop for some bags and they will often give them to you for free.

YOU WILL NEED

6 or more paper bags

Glue stick

Scissors

Masking tape

Wool or string

INSTRUCTIONS

1. Take the first paper bag and glue an upside-down 'T' shape along the bottom of the bag, and then straight up the middle.

2. Make sure you don't glue on the part of the bag that sticks out – like on the bag pictured where you can see the edge of the other side.

3. Place the next bag directly on top of the first and repeat the upside-down 'T' shape on this one too. Add the next four bags in the same way.

4. Cut a large arrow shape into the top edge of the glued-together bags. The closer to the bottom this cut goes, the wider the star will open.

5. Now you can unfurl your star!

6. Make a loop of masking tape with the sticky side out and join together the last two edges. You could also glue it but I prefer to use masking tape because it means that I can fold the star up and use it again.

7. Cut a small slit through the masking taped area.

8. Thread some wool or string though and it's ready to hang!

MATERIALS

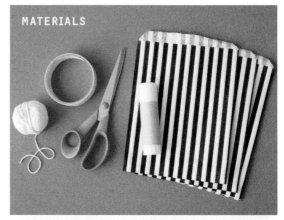

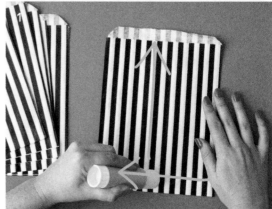

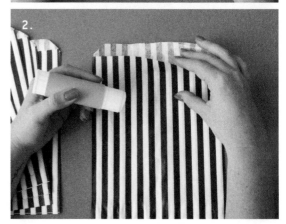

FORK POMPOM
GARLAND   ♡♡

Did you know that you can make
a pompom with a fork? It's a quick
way to make a mini pompom.

We made a few, then joined them all
together in a garland which looks
pretty when you hang it around
a mirror or a window.

Wool

Dental floss

A fork

Small scissors

INSTRUCTIONS

1. Start by winding some wool around a fork, leaving the gaps at the bottom. Make sure you don't let it unravel off the end of the fork.

2. Thread some dental floss through the middle gap at the bottom of the fork. This will be the thread that holds the pompom together. I use dental floss because it is incredibly strong so you can pull it very tight.

3. *GROWN-UP JOB* Tie the dental floss tightly around the wool. This is a grown-up job because it needs to be really tight. Get a helper to place their finger on the knot and tie a double knot.

4. Keep the dental floss ends long; these will help you to tie it onto the garland later.

5. Using the small scissors, cut the wool on one side of the fork. It will spring up like a pompom. Cut the other side as well. Slide it off the fork.

6. Trim the stray bits to neaten it up and make it spherical.

7. Make as many pompoms as you want! Use the dental floss threads to tie the pompoms onto a long piece of wool to make a garland.

8. Now you have a long garland of pompoms!

MATERIALS

1.

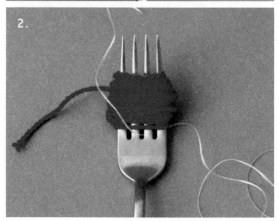

2.

PAPER CIRCLE BUNTING ⏰⏰

Bunting is usually made of triangles, but what if we made it from circles? This is super easy because you can use plates as circle templates.

It's perfect if you have a specific colour scheme that you want to create, or you could try it with rainbow colours to make lots of little rainbows.

YOU WILL NEED

3 x colours of tissue paper

3 x sizes of circular plates or bowls
to trace around

String

Pencil

Scissors

Stapler

INSTRUCTIONS

1. Choose the tissue paper colour that you want
   to be the largest circle. Trace around the
   largest plate (I used a dinner plate) using
   a pencil.

2. Cut out the tissue paper circle. I usually cut
   about 4 layers of tissue paper at once, which
   is handy if you have to make lots of circles.
   Small people might only be able to manage
   one layer at a time.

3. Choose your next colour and trace around
   the smaller plate (I used a side plate).

4. On your last colour, trace around your
   smallest plate or bowl. Cut out as before.

5. Layer the circles centred on top of each
   other. I used two layers of each colour for
   each bunting.

6. Fold the layered circle in half so it looks
   like a rainbow.

7. Put some string through the middle,
   making sure that it is close to the folded
   seam inside.

8. Staple in the centre of the semi-circle,
   making sure that the string is inside.
   Now repeat for all of your semi-circles.
   Make as much as you like!

MATERIALS

1.

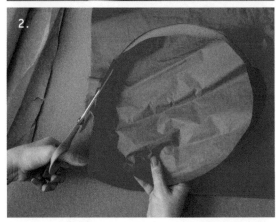

2.

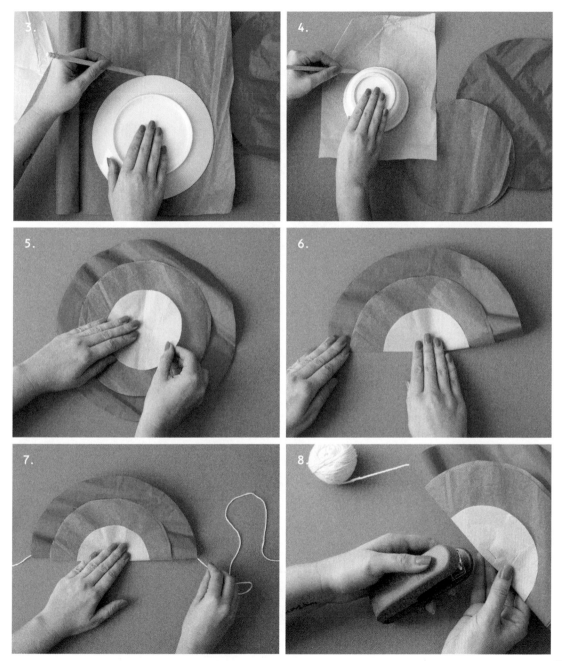

SILHOUETTE CAMEO

If you're good with scissors, you can make one of these silhouette cameos to hang on your wall. It's a great way to capture a moment in time forever.

The most important thing to get right is the photo. You can take it on your phone, but make sure the background is completely plain. The camera has to be straight, and make sure you take an exact side profile.

You could take a photo of a sibling or a grandparent ... or even a pet if you can get them to sit still!

YOU WILL NEED

A print-out of a photo on A4 paper (not photo paper, you need to be able to see through it)

Black paper (paper is better than card because it is easier to cut small details in paper)

A4 sheet of coloured backing paper

Scissors

Lead pencil

Glue

Picture frame

INSTRUCTIONS

1. Turn over your print-out and colour in the back in lead pencil. Make sure the silhouette is very darkly coloured with lead pencil.

2. Place the black paper under the print-out.

3. Trace around the edge of the photo person with the pencil, pressing hard. This will make the lead on the back of the page rub off onto the black paper.

4. You will now have an outline on the black paper. You might need to go over it with the pencil so it is more visible.

5. Carefully cut out the silhouette, including any little bits of hair. You could use nail scissors for the tiny bits.

6. Put some glue on the back of the silhouette.

7. Glue it onto a piece of backing paper and then it is ready to frame!

MATERIALS

1.

2.

3.

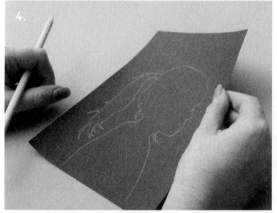

4.

5.

6.

7.

MAGIC STAR

What makes this star magic? It can hold itself together without any glue or string. If you find the magic combination, you can weave the sticks together and they will stay in the star formation.

This is a great way to learn about structure, geometry and tension. I have made my sticks different colours so it's easier to see the order to lay them down and how they overlap.

Once you've made your star, you could add some pompoms (from page 134) and some tassels (from page 114) and hang it up as a colourful decoration.

YOU WILL NEED

5 x bamboo skewers

Felt-tip pens

Scissors

String — if you want to hang it up

INSTRUCTIONS

1. Cut off the pointy ends of the skewers with scissors, so they aren't too sharp

2. Colour them with felt-tip pens.

3. Start with one skewer (yellow) laid horizontally across.

4. Place two more skewers (green) on top to form a capital A. At the apex, the right skewer lies on top of the left.

5. Add another skewer (orange); carefully lift the bottom left of the green skewer pictured, and place the orange skewer underneath. Then carefully lift the right side of the yellow skewer and place the orange end under it.

6. Now for the tricky bit. Place the final (pink) skewer on top of the other skewers as shown. Carefully place your hand on the whole star and gently slide the bottom end of the pink skewer under the bottom right green skewer. Then slide the top end of the pink skewer under the left side of the yellow skewer. This should hold it in place.

7. Make sure all the corner apexes have enough length just beyond each cross-over to hold it.

8. Now you should be able to pick up your magic star as one piece!

   If you want to hang it up as a decoration, I recommend tying string around the points so it doesn't pop undone.

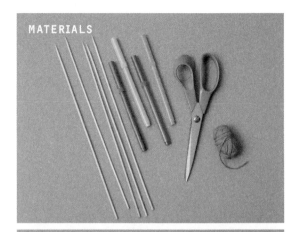

MATERIALS

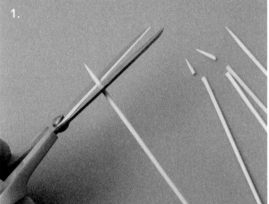

1.

2.

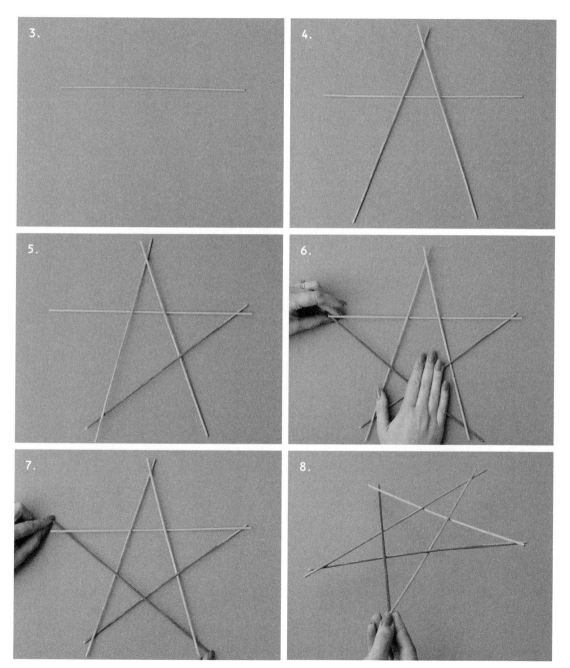

RAG WALL
HANGING 🕐🕐🕐

If you've got some T-shirts, tights
or leggings that you no longer need,
it's easy to make them into a cute
wall hanging.

Jersey fabric will turn into little
tubes when you cut it into strips,
which makes it perfect for
this project.

This is a great project to learn
about symmetry and repetition.

YOU WILL NEED

Old T-shirts, tights or leggings

Drinking straw that doesn't have a bendy bit

Masking tape

String

Scissors

INSTRUCTIONS

1. Cut some strips of fabric, about 1.5cm wide. Don't worry if they are a bit messy and cut them as long as you can. *The strips will be doubled over, which means that when they are hanging on your wall they will be half the length that they are now.*

2. Pull the strips so they will curl up on the sides to make tube shapes.

3. Lay out the strips in a symmetrical pattern. Add equal numbers of each colour on each side and put the longest in the middle.

4. Put some masking tape on the end of your straw. This will help to stop the fabric strips from sliding off the end.

5. Take a fabric strip, fold it over, then loop it around the straw as you see in the photo. You will end up with two equal pieces dangling off the straw. Add all the strips, one by one.

6. Carefully trim your strips into an arrow shape using scissors. It helps if it is lying flat on the table when you do this.

7. Carefully take the masking tape off the straw. Thread the string through the straw.

8. Tie the ends of the string together and use it to hang it on the wall.

MATERIALS

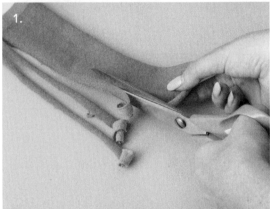

1.

2.

MOON PHASE BANNER

Have you ever noticed that the texture of a sponge looks a little bit like the surface of the moon? For this project we used sponges to make a banner showing the moon phases.

You need seven circles to show the moon phases, but it's a good idea to print more than seven so you can pick your favourites for the final banner.

YOU WILL NEED

Black paper or cardboard

A sponge with a large bubbly texture

String

White paint

Pencil

Scissors

Tape

Plate

INSTRUCTIONS

1. Draw seven circles on the black paper with a pencil using a roll of tape as a guide.

2. Draw a circle on the sponge too, then cut it out.

3. Put some white paint on a plate and dab the sponge onto it until it is evenly coated with paint. Carefully press the sponge on one of the circles on the paper to make a 'full moon'.

4. Now cut the sponge in half.

5. Press the half sponge into the paint and print two half moons onto the circles.

6. Now cut the sponge again to form the slimmer shape of a crescent moon.

7. Print the crescent moon onto the circles on the page. You need two of these, as shown.

8. Cut out all your moons, including two completely black ones for the 'new' moons. Arrange the moons in the order shown here.

9. Tape the back of each moon. I did mine as a vertical banner; you could also make it horizontal, like bunting. Then hang it against a wall.

JAPANESE FISH KITE

This is my version of a traditional Japanese kite called a Koinobori. Koinobori are made to celebrate Children's Day on 5 May and they are hung outside to flutter in the wind.

This is one of the more detailed projects in this book. It's a good choice for a rainy-day activity when you have a bit more time.

YOU WILL NEED

Tissue paper – any colour you like

Loo roll inner tube

White dot stickers for the eyes

Bamboo skewer

Glue stick

Scissors

Tape

String

Pen

INSTRUCTIONS

1. Cut a ring off the end of the loo roll tube that is about 1cm wide.

2. Cut a piece of tissue paper about 18cm x 25cm. Glue down the left-hand edge of the sheet of tissue paper

3. Roll the paper around the ring, leaving about 1.5cm of tissue paper hanging over the edge.

4. Fold this edge piece in so it sticks to the inside of the cardboard ring.

5. Flatten the body of the fish so you have two layers of tissue paper with a folded edge at the top and an opening at the bottom.

6. Cut out a fish shape: Start with the tail shape on the end; then cut indents to create the tail shape. You could draw the shape on first with pencil if you need to.

7. Glue along the edges of each piece of tissue paper. Then press them together to make a fish-shaped tube.

Continued on the next page ...

MATERIALS

1.

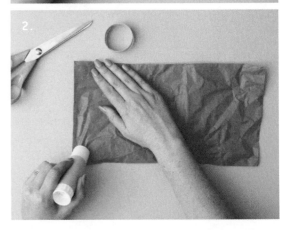

2.

8. Cut two small squares of tissue paper about 10cm x 10cm. Fold them into concertinas as shown.

9. Cut a curve off the corner of the concertina; when you open it, you will have a scalloped edge to make fins.

10. Glue the straight edge of the fin.

11. Pinch the end to make a gathered fin shape.

12. Glue the fins to the sides of the fish.

13. To make the eyes, draw a pupil on the white circle stickers – or cut a piece of white paper into a circle and draw a pupil on that. I like to do Pac-Man style eyes because they look quite graphic.

14. Cut two pieces of string, each about 15cm long. Tape a piece to either side of the mouth, sticking the string to the cardboard tube.

15. Tie your fish to the stick. I tied each one a few times so it was very well attached. Now make as many fish as you like and wave them in the wind!

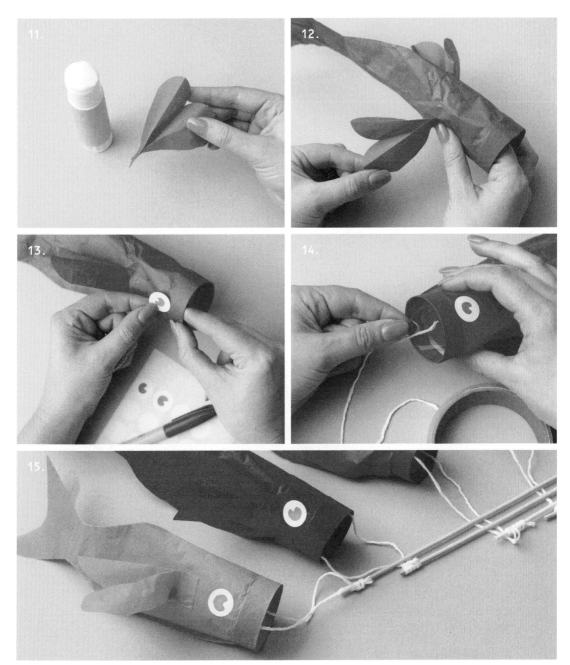

MILK BOTTLE BABOONS ♨ ♨

....

These funny baboons are made of plastic milk bottles and a grassy plant for their hair. They make great planters that you can hang on the wall. I used permanent markers to make the baboon face; red, blue and black will make a classic baboon, or if you only have a black marker, that looks effective too.

YOU WILL NEED

Grassy plant

Plastic milk bottle — it needs to have the handle placed symmetrically on the side of the bottle. It looks good to have a red lid for a mouth if possible

Permanent markers — black, red and blue

Scissors

Hole punch

INSTRUCTIONS

1. Draw a semi-circle as shown above the forehead using a black marker pen.

2. On the side, draw a shape for the ear, then a line up towards the back, as shown. Draw this on the other side too.

3. Draw a big curve around the back.

4. ***GROWN-UP JOB*** Cut the bottle around the line, so that the top section comes off.

5. Draw some straight lines to make the forehead. My bottle had embossed lines on there already that I followed and extended.

6. Now draw the eye area. Start with the eye shapes on either side of the handle.

7. Now draw a black mask shape around the eyes — a bit like a Batman mask — then colour it in.

8. Draw the eyes on. I also gave him a bottom eyelid, to look more baboon-like.

Continued on the next page ...

MATERIALS

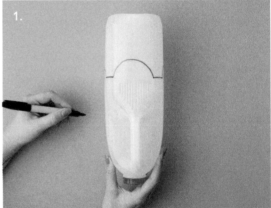

1.

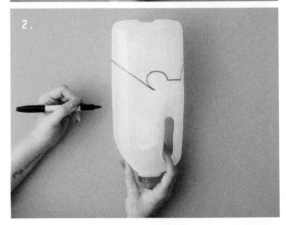

2.

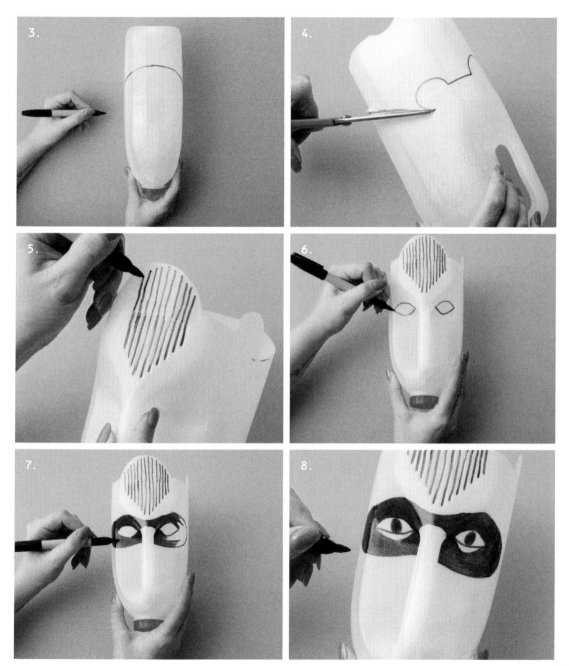

9. Colour the handle in red to make the nose. I coloured it all the way around the handle. It gets a little bit fiddly, so this part takes some time.

10. Draw on some nostrils at the bottom of the nose.

11. Draw the distinctive blue cheek markings that make it look like a baboon.

12. Draw semi-circles around the ear shapes.

13. Fold the ears to bend them outwards so that they stick out when you look at him from the front.

14. Now you can plant the grassy plant in the bottle. It's a good idea to put some stones or gravel in the bottom to help with drainage, like you would for a pot plant.

15. If you want to hang your baboon on a wall, make a small hole in the back in the centre with a hole punch.

16. Now you can hang him up on a wall.

17. If you want to hang him up using string, punch a hole in the front and fold out the forehead flap. Then hang him.

Make sure you water your baboon regularly according to the directions on the plant pot. Mine dried out a bit (I'm rubbish at keeping plants alive!) but they still look great because the dried grass looks extra baboony.

CHAPTER 4

USEFUL THINGS

Projects to make things
that you can use

BOB THE PYJAMA FISH

Tidying up just got a whole lot more
fun with Bob, the pyjama fish.
He likes to eat pyjamas. You can
hang him on the back of your door
and you'll always know where your
pyjamas are. You could also use him
to store your dirty laundry.
He'll eat that too.

He's made of an adult sized T-shirt
and a coathanger. The strips of
fabric at the bottom are all tied
together, so there's no sewing
involved at all.

YOU WILL NEED

1 x T-shirt

1 x wire coathanger

2 x polystyrene balls

2 x thumb tacks

Scissors

PVA glue

Black marker

INSTRUCTIONS

1. Cut the hem edge off the bottom of the T-shirt and both of the sleeves. And also cut the tag out from the neck.

2. Cut strips along the bottom of the T-shirt. I used an adult T-shirt and the strips were 12cm long and 1.5cm wide.

3. Cut similar strips on the sleeves.

4. Tie the front and back strips together using double knots. When the bottom of the T-shirt is enclosed like a bag, do the same to the sleeves.

5. Bend the wire coathanger into a circle.

6. Make a small hole about 4cm from the back of the neck of the T-shirt. Poke the coathanger hook through the hole. Put the rest of the coathanger through the neck, inside the T-shirt.

7. On either side of the neck hole, poke the thumb tacks through the T-shirt from the inside to attach the eyes.

8. Draw some black dots on the balls for pupils, then put a blob of PVA glue on the pin of each thumb tack and pierce the eyeball onto the point. Leave it flat until it is completely dry before you hang it up. Then he will be ready to eat your pyjamas!

MATERIALS

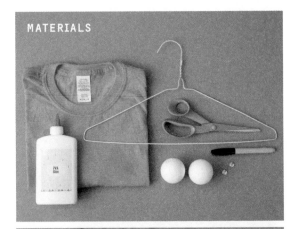

1.

2.

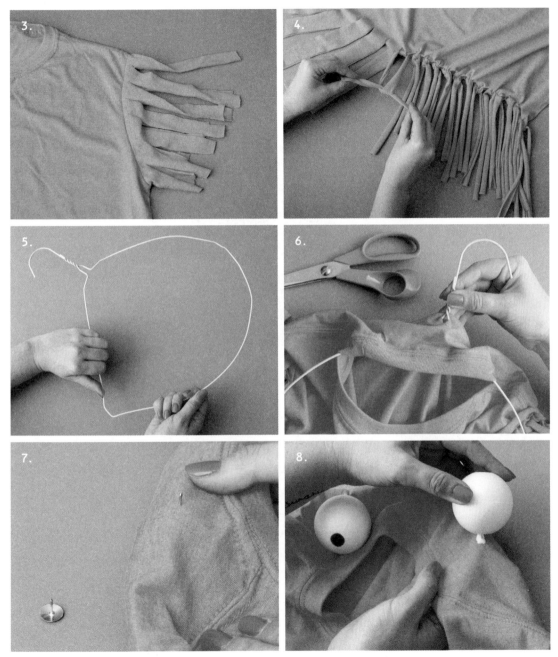

STINK THIEF

Sometimes creative projects come from a need to solve a problem.
I was having a look for a quick remedy for stinky shoes and found that
bicarbonate of soda is a great way to absorb the stink. A sachet of bicarb
in the shoes overnight will make the stink magically disappear.

So, if we give him a face and make him look like a little thief, he will
steal the stink away in the night. A great gift for any kids or grown-ups
who might have stinky shoes!

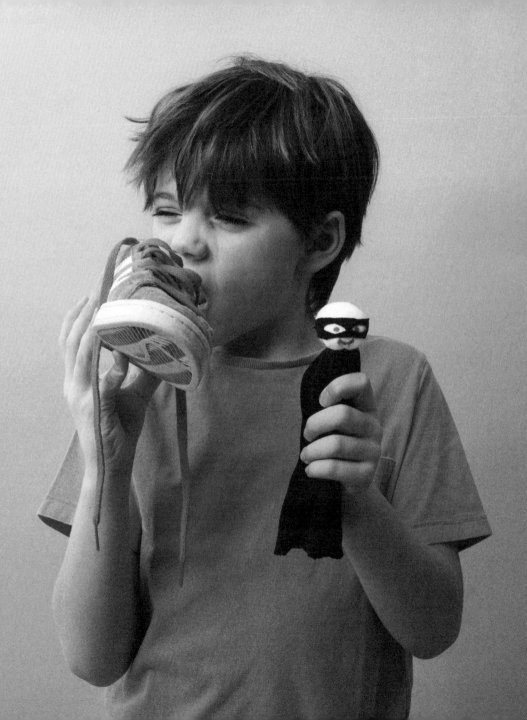

YOU WILL NEED

A wet wipe – dried out – I did this by leaving it out for 24 hours

1 tablespoon of bicarbonate of soda

Black tights or leggings

2 x elastic bands

Black marker pen

Scissors

INSTRUCTIONS

1. ***GROWN-UP JOB*** Put the bicarbonate of soda in the centre of the wet wipe. (It can sting if it gets in your eyes, which is why this is a grown-up job, but older children would be able to manage it.) Wash your hands afterwards.

2. Gather the wipe together, then tie an elastic band around to keep the powder from leaking out. This will be the head.

3. Cut a tube of tights or leggings about 25cm long.

4. Place the bundle inside the tube so that the head is halfway through the tube.

5. Wrap the second elastic around the neck and the tights fabric.

6. Pull the tights back to reveal the head. You will now have a head and body.

7. Draw on a cheeky face with the marker pen.

8. Cut a little bandit mask from the remaining tights or leggings fabric. Cut little eye holes, then tie it around the head.

9. Now pop him, head first, in a stinky shoe, and he will magically take the stink away.

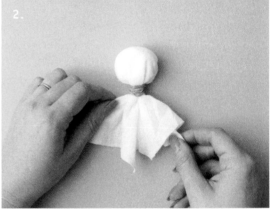

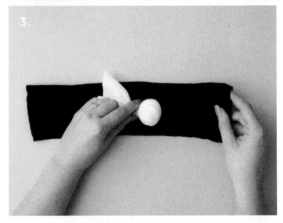

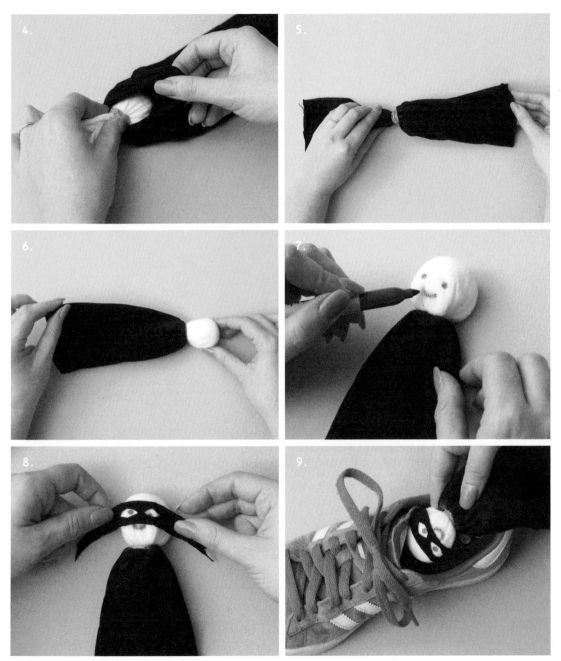

EGG HATS

These little egg hats will keep your egg warm while you
butter your toast. You could draw faces on your eggs
to give them character too. Choose from a clown,
a king and Señor Huevos Sombrero — or all three
if you're really hungry.

YOU WILL NEED

Sheets of felt – I got mine from the newsagent

Eggs

Scissors

Stapler

Glue stick

Black felt-tip pen

A plate, plus some other circle shapes to use as templates

INSTRUCTIONS

HUEVOS SOMBRERO

1. Use a side plate to mark out a semi-circle on the felt.

2. Cut out the semi-circle.

3. Make the semi-circle into a cone shape and test it out on your egg – remember that the edge will fold up.

4. Staple the cone about halfway down to join the edges together.

5. Fold the rim of the hat up to form the sombrero shape.

6. Add another staple to the rim of the hat to hold it together.

7. Now pop the sombrero on the egg. Draw a little face using the felt-tip pen.

Continued on the next page ...

HUEVOS SOMBRERO

1.

2.

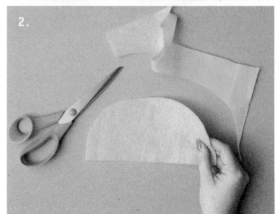

KING EGG

1. Cut a strip of felt — about 4cm x 15cm. Cut some zigzags along one length as shown.

2. Wrap a piece of felt around your egg to find the right size for the hat. Staple it together with two staples, where it joins.

3. Now pop it on the egg and draw a face.

HAPPY CLOWN EGG

1. Cut two semi-circles of different coloured felt. To cut the circles I traced around a CD for the small one and a small bowl for the large one. Trim to make a wedge shape. Cut out two small circles for buttons.

2. Roll the wedges into a cone and test it out on the egg to make sure it's the right size.

3. Staple the edges together through the two layers.

4. Fold the larger edge up and staple the edges together there too.

5. Glue on your buttons.

6. Put it on your egg, and draw a little face.

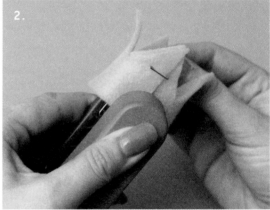

HAPPY CLOWN EGG

1.

2.

3.

4.

5.

6.

JUNK KEYRINGS

⏰ ⏰

We've all got bits of toy junk lying around, like beads, plastic characters and bits of things that will never find their partners. I thought it would be great to stack these up like absurd little sculptures, and turn them into something useful, like keyrings.

This project is great for parents who are confident using a drill. You'll need to drill through the pieces to create the holes that thread them together. Plastic, wood and rubber objects are best; avoid glass and metal.

YOU WILL NEED

Some toy junk bits

Metal keyring loop

String

Drill

Drill bit — I used 5mm

Pliers

A cardboard box (to use as a plinth when drilling, or a woodworking bench if you've got one)

INSTRUCTIONS

1. Arrange your junk into a little stack. Experiment with how the different objects stack together.

2. ***MAJOR GROWN-UP JOB!!*** Use the cardboard box as a plinth to do your drilling. You will need pliers to hold the object; don't attempt to do this with your bare hands!

3. Drill through the objects.

4. Make sure the holes in all the objects are big enough to thread the string through twice.

5. Thread the string through the holes. To make this easier, use a toothpick; tape the string to the toothpick so it works like a needle.

6. Once the string is through all the objects, loop it through the keyring loop, then back through all of the objects.

7. Now that all the objects are threaded on, knot the string securely.

8. Finish it off by tying a tassel at on on the end. (See how to make a tassel on page 114.) The thickness of the tassel will stop the toys coming off the end.

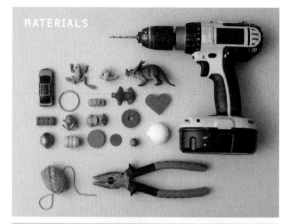

MATERIALS

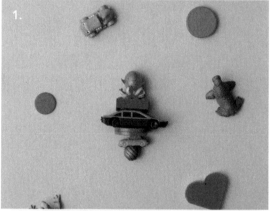

1.

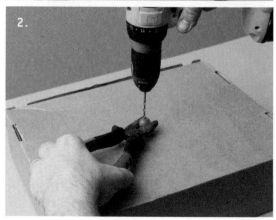

2.

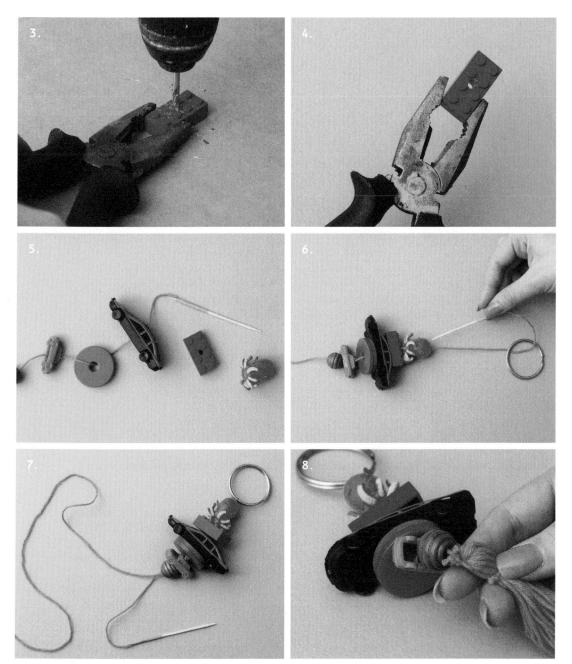

THANK YOU

As a grown-up I have been designing books and magazines for over fifteen years, but this is the first time that my name has appeared on the cover, it feels quite surreal!

The first book I ever made was called *What is Green?* and was first published in 1987 as a limited edition one off. It was about ten pages long and featured holes cut out of the pages revealing a green foil Quality Street wrapper that I had glued onto the back page. My mum told me it was fabulous and kept it in our bookcase alongside her hefty fine art books and my love for creating books was cemented. So I'd like to say a huge thanks to my mum for nuturing my love of books and always making time to be creative together.

Thanks to my kids, Elliot and Frida who have brought back the joy of making odd little things out of scraps for no reason. To my husband Tom, for unfalteringly supporting me in all my creative quests, however odd they seem and to the original Ladyland gang where it all started, Selina, Bella, Margherita, Celia, Clementine, Ruth and Kelly.

To Sam and Emma and the team at Penguin and Flora at Independent for all their support and hard work and the dream team at Junction Studio, Tom, Helena, Zoe, Sam, Anna and Mary – and to my friend Hollie for nudging me in a very fortuitous direction.

To my assistant Josie for all her meticulous work, for patiently cutting, sticking and shooting – and being a deft sushi chef.

And most importantly my little models, Frida, Elliot, Jessica, Louisa, Kate, Yousuf, Farah, Leilah and Louie. Thanks for helping me make the crafts and for bringing them to life with your lovely lovely faces.

10 9 8 7 6 5 4 3 2

Vermilion, an imprint of Ebury Publishing,
20 Vauxhall Bridge Road,
London, SW1V 2SA

Vermilion is part of the Penguin Random House group of companies whose addresses can be found at global.penguinrandomhouse.com

Penguin
Random House
UK

First published by Vermilion in 2019
www.penguin.co.uk

A CIP catalogue record for this book is available from the British Library

Design: Emma Scott-Child
Photography: Emma Scott-Child

ISBN: 9781785042485

Colour Reproduction: Altaimage Ltd, London
Printed and bound in Italy by L.E.G.O. S.p.A.

Penguin Random House is committed to a sustainable future for our business, our readers and our planet. This book is made from Forest Stewardship Council® certified paper.

MIX
Paper from
responsible sources
FSC® C018179